Ju 88
KAMPFGESCHWADER
ON THE WESTERN FRONT

SERIES EDITOR: TONY HOLMES

OSPREY COMBAT AIRCRAFT • 17

Ju 88

KAMPFGESCHWADER

ON THE WESTERN FRONT

John Weal

OSPREY
AVIATION

Front cover
On the afternoon of 27 September 1940, 55 Ju 88s of I. and II./KG 77 took off from Laon-Athies, in north-eastern France to attack south London. Despite missing the rendezvous with their fighter escort, the bombers pressed on, only to be met by some 120 Spitfires and Hurricanes. The Junkers' faultless formation was soon in tatters as they sought – singly or in small groups – to escape the RAF fighters. Twelve of the raiders failed to return, including 5./KG 77's Ju 88A-1 '3Z+HN' (Wk-Nr 7112), flown by *Staffelkapitän* Günther Zetzsche, which was shot down by Hurricane I 'RE-H' (P3710) of No 229 Sqn.

At the controls of the British fighter was Flg Off Vernon Bright, who also claimed a He 111 destroyed and a Bf 109E probably destroyed on this day. Although it appears that no other pilots were given credit for the Ju 88's demise, Bright was only officially awarded a third of a kill upon his return to Northolt – indeed, it is possible that this victory may have originally been listed as a 'probable'.

A veteran of the Battle of France and Operation *Dynamo* (the Dunkirk evacuation), not to mention count-less engagements over southern England since the commencement of the Battle of Britain, Bright dealt a series of mortal blows to the unescorted Ju 88 as it fled for the coast. The bomber eventually crashed into the Channel some 15 miles off Bexhill at 1600 hours, local time. There were no survivors amongst its four-man crew of Hauptmann Günther Zetzsche, Feldwebel W Mahl, Gefreiter A Burkhardt and Obergefreiter Alfred Kuhn. Indeed, only the body of the latter individual was ever located, being washed up near Walton-on-the-Naze on 30 October.

Having scored four and four shared destroyed, one unconfirmed destroyed, one probable and one damaged, Vernon Bright (who was by then a squadron leader) was himself killed two years later – almost to the day – on 24 September 1942 at the age of 26. The circumstances surrounding his death remain unrecorded
(*cover artwork by Iain Wyllie*)

First published in Great Britain in 2000 by Osprey Publishing
Elms Court, Chapel Way, Botley, Oxford, OX2 9LP

ISBN 1 84176 020 X

Edited by Tony Holmes
Page design by TT Designs, T & B Truscott
Cover Artwork by Iain Wyllie
Aircraft Profiles by John Weal
Scale Drawings by Mark Styling
Origination by Grasmere Digital Imaging, Leeds, UK
Printed through Bookbuilders, Hong Kong

00 01 02 03 04   10 9 8 7 6 5 4 3 2 1

EDITOR'S NOTE

To make this best-selling series as authoritative as possible, the editor would be interested in hearing from any individual who may have relevant photographs, documentation or first-hand experiences relating to aircrews, and their aircraft, of the various theatres of war. Any material used will be credited to its original source. Please write to Tony Holmes at 10 Prospect Road, Sevenoaks, Kent, TN13 3UA, Great Britain, or by e-mail at tony.holmes@osprey-jets.freeserve.co.uk

ACKNOWLEDGEMENTS

The author wishes to thank the following individuals for their invaluable assistance in providing photographs for use in this volume; Messrs Dr Alfred Price and Robert Simpson, and *Herren* Manfried Griehl, Holger Nauroth and Walter Stiebl. Finally, Osprey also acknowledges the provision of photographs from the Aerospace Publishing archive.

For a catalogue of all titles published by Osprey Publishing please contact us at:
Osprey Direct UK, P.O. Box 140, Wellingborough, Northants NN8 4ZA, UK
E-mail: **info@ospreydirect.co.uk**
Or visit our website: **www.ospreypublishing.com**

CONTENTS

1939-40 – THE *WUNDERBOMBER* YEARS

'You still owe me an aircraft carrier!' the Reichsmarschall boomed, only half-jokingly, as he caught sight of the familiar, white-overalled figure of Carl Francke.

The Luftwaffe Commander-in-Chief was making one of his periodic tours of inspection of the Rechlin test centre to watch the latest designs of the German aircraft industry being put through their paces. Francke, a leading test pilot at the Rechlin establishment, smiled his appreciation at his superior's heavy-handed witticism. If truth be told, however, he was heartily sick of such remarks. After all, he had never claimed to have sunk the *Ark Royal.*

It was the Propaganda Ministry which had elevated his near miss into an outright sinking. But Francke was not about to sour Göring's present mood of joviality by trying to convince him of the true facts.

It had all begun almost exactly a year before the outbreak of war when the then Generalfeldmarschall Hermann Göring was on an earlier visit to the Junkers aircraft factory. By that time the Luftwaffe was irrevocably committed to becoming a wholly tactical air force, whose main role was to support the army in the field. Indeed, the lone voice championing the development of a four-engined heavy bomber for the Luftwaffe had been stilled when Generalleutnant Walther Wever, Chief of the General Air Staff, died in an air crash. And along with Wever, who had been at the controls of the Heinkel He 70 courier aircraft which plunged into the ground shortly after taking off from Dresden airport on the morning of 3 June 1936, had perished not only his flight-engineer, but also the Luftwaffe's last chance of possessing a viable, long-range strategic bombing arm.

Wever's successors were all staunch advocates of tactical air power, who thought solely in terms of dive-bombers and twin-engined medium bombers. And no machine fitted the latter bill more perfectly than the *Schnellbomber* – or

The first prototype Ju 88 V1, powered by two 1000-hp Daimler Benz DB 600Aa engines, first flew on 21 December 1936. After only a few weeks it was lost in an accident during high-speed flight testing

Test pilots Ernst Siebert and Kurt Heintz in front of the 1200-hp Junkers Jumo 211B-1 engined record-breaking fifth prototype

high-speed bomber – currently under development at Junkers' Dessau works.

So impressed was Göring by this new aircraft that within days of his visit he had written to Junkers' managing director, Dr Heinrich Koppenberg, granting him full authority to begin series production at once. This missive, dated 3 September 1938, ended with the words, 'And now build me a mighty bomber fleet of Ju 88s in the shortest time possible'.

The Junkers Ju 88 was undoubtedly an excellent design, well deserving of the term *Wunderbomber* which was soon bestowed upon it. The first prototypes were unarmed, the original intention being that the Ju 88 – like the RAF's later Mosquito bomber – would rely entirely on its superior speed to escape the attention of enemy fighters. In March 1939 the fifth prototype demonstrated the Ju 88's potential when it established a new world air speed record for its class, completing a 1000-km (621-mile) closed circuit between Dessau and the *Zugspitze* – Germany's highest Alpine peak – at an average speed of 517 kmh (321 mph).

But mass-production of the Ju 88 in the 12 months following Göring's

Despite impressive propaganda shots such as this, production of the Ju 88 was protracted and slow. These are fuselages of the A-4 variant, development of which began early in 1940

letter of September 1938 did not go entirely according to plan. In fact, it hardly went at all. The prototypes which had made such an impression on the Generalfeldmarschall had been far from ready to enter series production. And to add to the usual assortment of teething troubles which inevitably beset any new design, reactionary elements within the RLM had since decreed that the *Wunderbomber* was to be equipped with defensive armament after all. Even more damaging was the decision to fit the Ju 88 with dive brakes, thereby allowing it to operate both as a high-speed level bomber *and* a dive-bomber.

The net result of this official tinkering with the basic design concept was not only a 65 kmh (40 mph)

A trio of early Ju 88A-1s from a training unit. Note the high demarcation line between upper and lower camouflage surfaces of the furthermost machine, and the small numerals on the tailfins. The snow on the ground would suggest that these are machines of *Lehrgruppe* 88, photographed in the winter of 1939-40

Walter Storp, who commanded I./KG 30's readiness flight at Westerland, pictured later in the war as a major, wearing the Oak Leaves to the Knight's Cross. In 1942 Storp became the first *Kommodore* of KG 6, and also served briefly as the *General der Kampfflieger*

reduction in maximum speed, but the dashing of Göring's hopes for a steady stream of deliveries of the new bomber to his operational units.

Thus, on 1 September 1939, in place of the expected 'mighty bomber fleet of Ju 88s', the Luftwaffe embarked upon World War 2 with exactly 12 examples of the Junkers' twin in first-line service.

The term 'first-line' was something of a misnomer, too. Only days earlier these dozen machines had formed part of the experimental *Erprobungskommando* 88, the unit tasked with testing the bomber under service conditions and evolving suitable training procedures. On the eve of hostilities 12 selected crews and their aircraft had been detached from *EKdo* 88 and transferred to Jever, where they were to operate under their newly appointed *Staffelkapitän*, Hauptmann Helmut Pohle, as 1./KG 25.

Forty-eight hours after Hitler's troops marched into Poland, Great Britain declared war on Germany. In immediate response on that same 3 September *Luftflotte* 2 – the command stationed in, and responsible for the defence of, north-western Germany – raised the status of one of its special-duties staffs (*Stab des Generals z.b.V.)* to that of a *Flieger-Division*.

Commanded by Generalleutnant Hans Ferdinand Geisler from his HQ at Blankenese on the banks of the River Elbe, 10. *Flieger-Division's* primary role was to be anti-shipping – more specifically, it was to seek out and destroy units of the Royal Navy in, and across, the North Sea. Geisler's main strike force was provided by the Heinkel He 111 bombers of KG 26, known as the 'Lion' *Geschwader*. But as over half that unit's strength was currently engaged in the offensive against Poland, the dozen Ju 88s of 1./KG 25 stationed at Jever were added to Geisler's Division to bolster its somewhat meagre order of battle.

The AOC of *Luftflotte* 2 had other ideas, however. *General der Flieger* Helmuth Felmy was firmly of the opinion that it would be a grave mistake to throw a new and untried unit, flying an aircraft still officially undergoing technical trials, piecemeal into battle in this way. He therefore ordered the withdrawal of 1./KG 25 back east to Greifswald in Pommerania, home-base of the *EKdo* 88, where a second operational *Staffel* of six Ju 88s – 2./KG 25 – was already forming.

On 7 September 1939 the short-lived KG 25 disappeared from Luftwaffe records when these two *Staffeln*, soon to be joined by a third, were redesignated to become I./KG 30. The new *Gruppe* began a hectic period of working up. But, as *Gruppenkommandeur* Hauptmann Helmut Pohle later explained; 'General Felmy did make one concession. He allowed a readiness flight to remain in the west. These four machines, commanded by Leutnant Walter Storp, transferred from Jever up to Westerland on the island of Sylt. The General promised that when the English fleet next put in an appearance, the readiness flight would not be left idle.

He rejected my suggestion that the whole *Gruppe* be used in any forthcoming action.'

The General was not simply keeping a tight rein on an overly eager subordinate. His strong convictions also prompted him to write to the High Command in Berlin urging restraint. The new Ju 88 should not be used in dribs and drabs, he cautioned. Patience should be exercised until at least a complete *Geschwader* – a minimum of 100 aircraft – was declared operational and ready to launch a mass attack.

But Göring would have none of it. This business with the Ju 88 had dragged on long enough already. The *Wunderbomber* needed a success to establish its reputation – and it needed it quickly. The opportunity was not long in coming.

On the morning of 26 September 1939 a Dornier Do 18 flying boat of 2.(F)/106 from Norderney was patrolling the North Sea. Suddenly, through a rift in the clouds, the observer spotted the tell-tale wake of a large ship travelling at speed. As the Do 18 continued to circle above the one break in the otherwise solid undercast, two more heavy ships hove into view.

The crew of the flying boat had stumbled across major units of the British Home Fleet. The battlecruisers *Hood* and *Renown*, accompanied by the aircraft carrier *Ark Royal*, together with a cruiser squadron and attendant destroyers, had been sent out to act as cover for a second cruiser squadron which was escorting the submarine *Spearfish* – badly damaged off the coast of Denmark and unable to dive – back across the North Sea. Also in the vicinity, providing deeper support, were the battleships *Nelson* and *Rodney*.

News of the sighting was radioed back to base, where no time was lost in alerting the bomber crews on Sylt. Their orders were succinct and explicit; 'Enemy located in grid square 4022. Long-range reconnaissance maintaining contact. Attack with 500-kg bombs'.

The first to take off, at 1250 hours local time, were nine He 111s of 4./KG 26. Some ten minutes later the four Ju 88s of I./KG 30's 'readiness flight' followed them into the air. Leutnant Walter Storp takes up the story;

'The crew were just going to lunch when a long-distance telephone call came in.

'"Emergency readiness!"

'I dashed across to the operations room. A reported enemy sighting; two English battlecruisers, an aircraft carrier and a number of small destroyers and torpedo-boats in the middle of the North Sea, roughly half-way between the east coast of Scotland and the Norwegian coast. Course westwards.

'Naturally, our main target is the carrier. We take off individually – one after the other. My orders are to approach at low level. And after only

A Ju 88A-1 of I./KG 30, the *Gruppe* which first took the *Wunderbomber* into action over the North Sea. It is pictured at dusk, presumably having just returned from such a mission. Note the extended underwing dive-brake. Although identified as aircraft '4D+BB' of the *Gruppenstab*, this machine wears the badge usually ascribed to 1. *Staffel* . . .

about an hour's flying we make contact. The first ships we see are a pair of cruisers. Arriving out of the sun we fly past them and realise, to our astonishment, that they haven't spotted us.

'Should we attack them? No, our main target is the aircraft carrier! We continue to head northwards.

'Look there! The carrier. Suddenly a tall column, grey-black and close alongside. That was the first bomb from the machine ahead of me.'

Flying that machine was Gefreite (Aircraftman First Class) Carl Francke.

The lowly military rank belied Francke's background and true abilities. In fact, he was a qualified engineer, aircraft technician and highly experienced civilian test pilot. As leader of the Ju 88's technical trials programme at Rechlin, he knew the aircraft inside out. But he was not only a skilled test pilot; he was a passionate flyer too. As a member of the German team at the 4th International Flying Meeting held at Zürich-Dübendorf in the summer of 1937, Dipl.-Ing. Carl Francke had won an individual speed record and the climb and dive competition in Bf 109 fighter prototypes.

The successful German contingent at Dübendorf had been led by Ernst Udet, then Director of the Technical Department of the RLM. Francke's close ties with the colourful Udet had no doubt smoothed his passage when, in August 1939, he volunteered for military service with *Erprobungskommando* 88 under the command of another old friend, Hauptmann Helmut Pohle.

Having exchanged his trademark white overalls for a regulation issue flying suit with a single stripe on each sleeve, and now rejoicing in the nickname of *'Biber'* ('Beaver') – a sly dig at his carefully nurtured and lovingly tended moustache – the erstwhile test pilot was a natural choice to captain one of the four Ju 88s awaiting their baptism of fire.

. . . and a closer look at the badge in question, which depicts Chamberlain's famous umbrella – a motif often used to represent England in Luftwaffe heraldry during the early months of the war – with a German bombsight superimposed. In this case, however, the bombsight itself appears to have been the target, as witness the ringed shrapnel damage caused by a near miss from an anti-aircraft shell

A contemporary newspaper portrait of Carl Francke published in mid-October 1939 and captioned; 'Promoted from Gefreite to Leutnant'. The bubble had yet to burst

On 26 September Gefreiter Francke had been number three to take off;

'We lifted off shortly before 1300 hours. As an experienced old aviation sea-dog, I flew at a height of 500 metres (1640 ft), for a thick bank of unbroken cloud stretched above us. At this altitude I had a better chance of spotting the enemy fleet.

'At the expected time, almost to the minute, the ships came into sight. Real heavyweights, just as reconnaissance had reported. As we were heading straight for them, I turned slightly to get into a better attacking position and climbed to 3000 metres (9840 ft). This took us above the cloud layer, which meant that the carrier was invisible as I commenced my dive. On breaking back down through the cloud it was immediately apparent that the attack would not be successful. The target was not centred in my sights.'

From his previous experiences at Rechlin, Francke was fully conversant not only with the Ju 88's capabilities, but also its limitations. He knew that he was too wide of the mark to be able to correct his course during the dive, and that there was no other option but to break off the attack and make a second attempt. As he climbed back towards the safety of the clouds, his mind registered the lack of response from the carrier.

In fact, members of the *Ark Royal's* crew had been watching Francke's movements with interest. They had mistaken the unfamiliar shape of the Junkers for that of a Lockheed Hudson, and were marvelling at the manoeuvrability of Coastal Command's new American twin. It was not until an able-seaman up on the range-finder pointed out to his officer that, 'Udsons don't 'ave bloody great crosses under their wings', that the penny dropped!

When Francke re-appeared out of the clouds some eight minutes later, the *Ark's* anti-aircraft gunners were ready and waiting;

'I initiated the second attack from 2700 metres (8856 ft). This time when I emerged from the clouds I was almost bang on target. A slight adjustment was all that was needed. The fire from the ship's flak made it stand out like some giant, illuminated advertising hoarding. But nothing hit us.

'At the correct altitude I pressed the bomb release button. The first bomb exploded in the water some 20 metres (65 ft) from the target, but the second hit the carrier on the starboard side.

'Unfortunately, at the moment of impact, I was fully occupied recovering from the dive, but the crew reported seeing a thick black cloud of smoke and signs of fire.

'Aircraft of the reconnaissance squadron kept a close watch on the carrier. Although it remained with the fleet, it was listing badly and apparently unable to hold a steady course.

'The next day, when the fleet was sighted again, the two battlecruisers were on their own and there was no sign of the aircraft carrier. It had disappeared.'

But the *Ark Royal* had not been sunk. Timing his move to perfection, her captain had ordered the helm spun hard over, which turned the ship out of the path of the falling 1000-lb bomb. The missile – which one officer likened to the 'size of a London bus' – exploded on impact with the sea less than five metres (15 ft) from the *Ark's* stem.

A huge wall of white water was thrown up. It came crashing down on the for'ard end of the flightdeck. The hull shuddered to the blast as the

Francke's nemesis. Instead of providing an early propaganda coup, the aircraft carrier HMS *Ark Royal*, seen here in the company of one of her escorting destroyers and a *Nelson*-class battleship, remained a thorn in the side of the Axis until her eventual sinking by U-81 in the Mediterranean in November 1941

carrier was lifted bodily upwards. She lurched viciously before settling. She did indeed take on a list to starboard, but this slowly righted itself until she was back on an even keel.

Vice-Admiral, Aircraft Carriers, Vice-Admiral L V Wells, who wore his flag in the *Ark*, was dismissive of the attack, saying that it amounted to 'no more than the breaking of a little crockery and splashing us with some water'.

Leutnant Walter Storp, who had witnessed the explosion of Francke's bomb, suffered even crueller luck. He scored a direct hit on the battle-cruiser *Hood*, but his bomb bounced off her armoured sides without detonating, the only evidence of its passage being a large patch of grey paint which flaked off to reveal the red lead underneath.

Meanwhile, the slower Heinkels of 4./KG 26 had found the nearby cruiser squadron, which they attacked at low level but failed to hit.

It was the signal Francke radioed back to base, carefully worded and only cautiously optimistic though it was, which was to prove his undoing; 'Dive-bombing attack on aircraft carrier with two SC 500 bombs; first, near miss close alongside; second, possible hit forward quarter. Results not observed.'

Anti-shipping operations over the North Sea at the beginning of the war set the pattern for a long-term partnership between the 'Eagle' and the 'Lion' *Geschwader*. Seen here in Norway in the spring of 1940, a II./KG 30 Ju 88 shares a field with a He 111 of 2./KG 26

This was enough for the Luft-waffe High Command in Berlin. When they received a copy of Francke's signal, they despatched their own reconnaissance flight that same afternoon. It, too, spotted the two battlecruisers, but failed to locate the carrier – just a fortuitous oil slick. The possibility that the British force may have split up seems to have occurred to no-one. The *Ark Royal* was declared sunk and the propaganda band-wagon began to roll.

But there were those who harboured doubts. Oberst Hans Siburg, the *Geschwaderkommodore* of KG 26, was an ex-navy man who was only too well aware that a column of smoke, and even a flash of flame, from an enemy ship did not necessarily mean that it had been hit. Such signs, more often than not, were an indication that the enemy vessel was firing her own guns.

Amidst all the confusion and excitement which surrounded the Junkers' return to Westerland, Siburg managed to have a quiet word with Francke. 'Did you actually see the carrier sink?' he enquired. Francke admitted quite candidly that he hadn't.

In Berlin, too, Generaloberst Hans Jeschonnek, Chief of the Luftwaffe General Staff, was also sceptical. That same afternoon he put through a call to Hauptmann Helmut Pohle, *Gruppenkommandeur* of I./KG 30 at Greifswald.

'Congratulations, Pohle. Your readiness flight at Westerland has just sunk the *Ark Royal!'*

The two men knew each other of old. Pohle could detect the doubt in Jeschonnek's voice, and replied without hesitation, 'I don't believe it'.

'Nor do I', agreed the Chief of Staff in his strong Berlin accent, 'but the *'Eiserne'* (the 'Iron One' – a reference to Göring) does. Get over to Westerland at once and find out the truth'.

When Pohle landed at Westerland later that evening, Francke was at his wits' end. Four weeks of military service went by the board as the aircraftman greeted the new arrival, not as his superior officer, but as a trusted friend, 'For heaven's sake, Pohle, none of this is true. Help me to get out of this mess!'

But it was too late. The following day a Wehrmacht communiqué announced to the whole world the sinking of the carrier. And Francke received a telegram;

'I congratulate you on your attack on the British aircraft carrier, which was carried out with great dash and crowned with well deserved success. For this superb feat of arms I, as your Luftwaffe Commander-in-Chief, promote you with immediate effect to the rank of Leutnant. For your outstanding bravery in the face of the enemy I award you, in the name of the Führer and the Supreme Commander of the Wehrmacht, the Iron Cross, Second and First Class.
Generalfeldmarschall Göring.'

Francke, the unwilling hero, became a household name. But as evidence emerged that the *Ark Royal* was still not only very much afloat, but also completely undamaged, his fortunes deteriorated even further. Not everybody was as philosophical about the affair as Göring appeared to be. Some of Francke's fellow officers were openly derisive of his promotion and the decoration he had been awarded for something he did not do. Francke returned to Rechlin to resume test flying, but continued to be dogged by the events of 26 September 1939.

Long before the *Ark* herself finally succumbed to a U-boat torpedo in the Mediterranean in November 1941, Francke had reached such a stage that he confided to a then still neutral American journalist that he was contemplating suicide. He obviously thought better of it, and volunteered instead for another operational posting – only to be killed later on the Eastern Front.

Francke's abortive attack on the *Ark Royal* meant that the Ju 88 had still not yet delivered the success Göring demanded of it. At this early stage of the war the only theatre of operations where such success might be achieved was the stretch of North Sea between Great Britain and Norway, an area which Luftwaffe pilots referred to as *'das nasse Dreieck'* – 'the wet, or watery, triangle'.

Two subsequent armed sweeps achieved nothing beyond the first confirmed loss of a Ju 88 to enemy action. A 3. *Staffel* machine was damaged by anti-aircraft fire from ships of the Royal Navy's Humber Force off the tip of Norway on 9 October and crashed into the sea shortly before reaching the safety of the German coast.

The Commander-in-Chief evidently decided that further encouragement was called for. On the morning after this latest incident the *Gruppenkommandeur* of I./KG 30 was summoned to attend a high level meeting at the RLM in Berlin. Göring's message was brief and to the point;

'Pohle, we have now *got* to have success. There are only a few English ships making things difficult for us. The *Repulse*, the *Renown*, perhaps the old *Hood* as well. And, of course, the carriers. But once these are out of the way, the navy's *Scharnhorst* and *Gneisenau* will dominate the seas out to the Atlantic Ocean.'

Helmut Pohle assured the Generalfeldmarschall that his pilots were only awaiting their chance. And this time he got his way. The whole of I./KG 30 would be moved up to Westerland and held at constant readiness.

The chance came within a week. On 15 October a reconnaissance aircraft on routine patrol spotted a British battlecruiser, thought to be the *Hood*, off the Scottish coast. Early the following morning the vessel was again sighted as it was about to enter the Firth of Forth. At 0930 hours Pohle received his orders over the telephone from Jeschonnek in Berlin. The Chief of Staff added a warning. On the 'personal instructions of the Führer', Pohle was on no account to attack the *Hood* if she was already berthed in the naval yards. With hostilities between Germany and Great Britain only just into their seventh week, it was still very much a 'gentleman's war'. Neither side's bombers were allowed to attack the other's ships once they were in dock, for fear of causing civilian casualties.

At 1100 hours Hauptmann Pohle took off from Westerland, leading his 15 Ju 88s on the two-hour flight across the North Sea;

'We flew in widely separated vics of three, as we had been told that there were no Spitfire squadrons in Scotland.'

But, as would prove to be the case all too often in the months to come, Luftwaffe intelligence was seriously at fault. In fact, there were at least three squadrons of Spitfires in the vicinity of the target area, plus another two of Gladiators. Pohle

This shot of a Ju 88A-1 shows clearly the *Lotfe* bombsight mounted in the ventral gondola, and the four external bomb carriers below the inboard wing sections

Having negotiated the entrance lock, the broad-beamed shape of a capital ship (arrowed), possibly the *Hood,* is safely docked in the Rosyth yard. This photograph was taken by a Luftwaffe reconnaissance aircraft

Just below the Firth of Forth railway bridge, the cruisers *Southampton* and *Edinburgh* are seen under attack by Pohle's Ju 88s. When this picture was first published in German newspapers, Inch Garvie Island – visible in the shadow of the centre span – was annotated as a column of smoke from a direct hit on the bridge! On this print an attempt has been made to delete the (a) marking the island

did have one stroke of luck, however. The local radar station had suffered a major power failure and the Ju 88s remained undetected until ground observers actually saw them flying overhead at 4000 metres (13,000 ft). RAF fighters were scrambled immediately, but Pohle had a few precious minutes to position his force for the attack.

Far below, the Forth bridge cast its unmistakable shadow across the sunlit waters of the firth. At its northern end, just upstream, lay the Rosyth naval dockyards. And there, securely penned in the entrance lock, was the equally unmistakable broad-beamed shape of a battlecruiser. The bombers were just too late.

'A stationary target. perfect for dive-bombing', Pohle later recounted ruefully, 'but we were strictly forbidden to attack this sitting duck'.

But there were other, legitimate, targets – including two cruisers and several destroyers – in the open water of the firth just below the bridge. Pohle selected one of the cruisers, the 9100-ton *Southampton*, and tipped the nose of his '*Anton-Kurfürst*' into a steep 80-degree dive.

'Suddenly, there was an almighty crack as the roof of the canopy flew off, taking the rear gun with it.'

Pohle was unsure whether the damage had been caused by enemy anti-aircraft fire or by structural failure – the latter had occurred more than once during dive tests at Rechlin, and would seem to indicate that not all the bugs had yet been ironed out of the Junkers. Despite the gale howling about his ears, Pohle held the machine rock-steady and planted his 500-kg (1102-lb) bomb squarely on the *Southampton*.

Like the bomb which had struck the *Hood* three weeks earlier, it failed to explode. Instead, it sliced cleanly through three of the *Southampton*'s decks before exiting through her flank and sinking a launch moored alongside. The *Wunderbomber* had claimed its first victim – although perhaps not quite of the calibre Göring had been hoping for!

As Pohle eased the bomber out of its near-vertical dive, his wireless-operator shouted a mortifying warning; 'A *Kette* of Spitfires are attacking!'

'I didn't have a chance to take any defensive action', Pohle later wrote, 'our left engine was hit almost immediately and began to smoke. I turned out to sea, hoping to reach the *Hörnum* – a rescue trawler which the navy had positioned off the Scottish coast.'

Luftwaffe's eye view – a low-level, but understandably less than sharp, photograph of HMS *Edinburgh* taken by one of the attackers as it pulled out of its near-vertical dive

The photographer photographed? Although of not much better quality, this surface shot clearly shows a Ju 88 levelling out after dropping a bomb near the *Edinburgh*. This picture, too, later found its way into the German press

'Still a gentleman's war'. Two of Pohle's crew are accorded full military honours – *Reichskriegs-flagge*-draped coffins and an RAF escort, plus a respectful salute from a bobby in the background – as they are carried to a cemetery near Edinburgh

But Pohle didn't make it. The three Spitfires, from No 602 Sqn (see *Aircraft of the Aces 12 - Spitfire Aces of World War 2* for further details) curved in for a second pass. Their combined fire killed two of his crew members and put the labouring port engine out of action altogether. The Junkers struggled on for another 12 miles (20 km), suffering further attacks which wounded the observer, before Pohle was forced to ditch in the sea off Fife Ness. He was the only one of the crew to survive; spending the next six years as a prisoner-of-war.

Leutnant Horst von Riesen underwent a very similar experience to his *Gruppenkommandeur*,

'During the dive a heavy flak shell must have exploded quite close to our machine. A loud bang momentarily drowned the sound of our engines, and then a strong wind howled through the cockpit. The right engine cowling had been blown off and the cabin canopy buckled inwards.'

Von Riesen nevertheless pressed home his attack, which damaged the destroyer *Mohawk*, before seeking the safety of open water. He, too, was pursued by Spitfires, but managed to limp back to Westerland on his one good engine. Meanwhile, some 45 minutes after Pohle's ditching, the defending fighters brought down a second Junkers when a section of Spitfires from No 603 Sqn shot 1. *Staffel's* 'Dora-Heinrich' into the firth four miles (six kilometres) north of Port Seton.

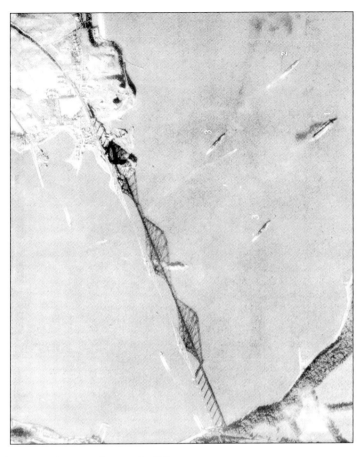

Taken from almost the same position as the earlier photograph of the attack on the two cruisers (and, to judge from the shadow, at almost the same time of day – albeit clearly from a greater altitude), this subsequent reconnaissance photo of the Firth has captured the unmistakable form of the aircraft carrier *Furious* (top right). But this time the Luftwaffe's photographic interpreters have left Inch Garvie strictly alone!

The following day, 17 October, four Ju 88s of I./KG 30, led by their new *Gruppenkommandeur*, Hauptmann Fritz Dönch, took off from Westerland to attack Scapa Flow, the Royal Navy's main base on the Orkney Islands. On arrival they found the anchorage all but deserted, the Home Fleet having been withdrawn to the safety of Loch Ewe on the west coast of Scotland following U-47's daring foray deep into the Flow only 72 hours earlier, which had resulted in the torpedoing and sinking of the battleship *Royal Oak*.

The sole vessel of any size remaining at Scapa was the unseaworthy *Iron Duke*, an ancient and partially stripped battleship which was moored close to the naval base on the island of Hoy. A near miss from one of the Junkers' bombs caused severe underwater damage, and the venerable *Duke* had to be towed into shallow water and beached. In return, anti-aircraft fire brought down one of the raiders.

RAF defences permitting, Luftwaffe reconnaissance aircraft kept a close watch on naval activity both in the Firth of Forth and at Scapa Flow. Wk-Nr 1333 of an unidentified recce *Staffel* has obviously been to Scapa, as evidenced by the name and map, but whether the 20 mission bars all refer to return visits to the anchorage by the same crew – or is a *Staffel* total – is unclear

The 2. *Staffel* machine, which exploded on Hoy, was the first Luftwaffe aircraft to physically crash on British soil in World War 2.

With the capital ships of the Home Fleet retired out of harm's way, I./KG 30 had to seek other targets. Despite the worsening weather – the winter of 1939-40 was to be the severest for many years – the *Gruppe* continued to mount the occasional armed sweep. Most of these proved inconclusive. But on 13 November, during a raid against military installations on the Shetland Islands, which included the RAF's flying-boat base at Sullom Voe, I./KG 30 played its own small part in escalating the new European air war by dropping the first bombs to fall on Great Britain since 1918. All four missiles exploded harmlessly in an open field – the only purported casualty being a rabbit. In fact, the unfortunate creature, whose picture was widely printed in the national press, was already deceased – it had been hurriedly purchased in the local butcher's shop and placed in one of the bomb craters for its propaganda effect!

Some five weeks later, on 22 December, two Ju 88s of I./KG 30 re-appeared over the Firth of Forth on a reconnaissance mission. They were met by their old adversaries, the Spitfire Is of No 602 Sqn, whose pilots inexplicably identified the raiders as Heinkel He 115 floatplanes! Although both Junkers managed to escape, one crashed on returning to base.

By this time a second operational *Gruppe* had been formed from a cadre supplied by the new Ju 88 instructional unit (*Lehrgruppe* 88), II./KG 30 being declared operational early in December 1939. The following month III./KG 30 was created in similar fashion. Both these *Gruppen*, together with the recently established *Geschwaderstab* under Oberstleutnant Walter Loebel (previously *Kommandeur* of I./KG 26), were initially based at Barth, on the Baltic coast. With KG 30 now at full establishment, and on a numerical par with KG 26, a clear division of labour was introduced. In the past weeks, small numbers of I./KG 30's Ju 88s had often operated in conjunction with larger formations of He 111s of the 'Lion' *Geschwader*. Now the latter were to concentrate primarily on merchant shipping, leaving the Ju 88s of the newly-fledged 'Eagle' *Geschwader* to attack the Royal Navy.

But for the first couple of months of 1940 I./KG 30 was to soldier on alone over the North Sea, suffering a series of individual losses in the process.

The first of these occurred on New Year's Day, when one of six Ju 88s despatched to the Orkney and Shetland areas failed to return. Another Junkers was lost on 3 February, the day on which machines of 2. *Staffel* finally scored the *Geschwader's* first confirmed success by attacking and sinking the 875-ton fleet minesweeper HMS *Sphinx* off the Moray Firth. Six days later I./KG 30 sunk two smaller minesweepers, both

Ju 88A '4D+AA' was the mount of Oberstleutnant Walter Loebel, the first *Geschwaderkommodore* of KG 30. Note that the background shield to the 'Diving Eagle' unit badge on *Geschwaderstab* machines was divided diagonally into the three *Gruppe* colours which were, from the top, red, white and yellow

converted trawlers, in the same region, but again at the cost of one of their number.

On 8 March thick cloud foiled a reconnaissance of Scapa Flow by three Ju 88s of I./KG 30. One was brought down by defending fighters some miles out to sea, although the remaining pair returned safely to Westerland, but with nothing to report. Although the bad weather over the islands had prevented the Junkers from confirming the fact, German suspicions that the British

Home Fleet was returning to its main base in the Orkneys were well founded. The battleship *Valiant* and the *Hood* had arrived at Scapa on 7 March, and two more battlecruisers, *Repulse* and *Renown*, accompanied by the battleship *Rodney*, followed 48 hours later.

Such a concentration of heavy ships, plus their accompanying cruisers and destroyers, could not remain undetected for long. As soon as their presence was discovered, an apprehensive German Naval Staff pressed the Luftwaffe to mount a full-scale bombing raid. It was carried out by a mixed force, the He 111s of KG 26 being ordered to suppress the ground defences, while I./KG 30's Ju 88s dive-bombed the ships anchored out in the Flow. The 18 Junkers were again led by *Gruppenkommandeur* Hauptmann Fritz Dönch;

Oberstleutnant Loebel (right) with a group of his pilots including, at centre in the flying helmet, Hauptmann Fritz Dönch, Gruppenkommandeur of I./KG 30. Judging by the rather set expressions of the flying-suited aircrew, this is a preflight briefing session rather than a triumphant return from a successful mission

'We did not fly to the target by the direct route, preferring a more roundabout approach to give us the element of surprise. The weather was still far from good. Rain and snow showers limited visibility. As we neared Scapa Flow, however, the weather gods smiled upon us. The clouds parted and in the fading evening light we could see the heavy ships far below us.'

Dönch ordered his formation to split into *Ketten* and select individual targets. At 2000 metres (6560 ft) the Ju 88s nosed over into their steep dives. The *Rodney* and *Renown* were among those subjected to attack.

'Everything went like clockwork. We had achieved complete surprise and were able to plant our bombs with great accuracy. Several ships received direct hits. Others suffered near misses, which must have caused severe damage.

'Although the flak grew in intensity during the course of the attack, only one pilot reported being hit, and he was able to return to base. Enemy fighters did not trouble us at all. By 1955 hours it was all over. The fires of the burning British ships remained visible long after we had set course for home.'

The crews received a rapturous welcome back at Westerland. They reported hits on three battleships and one heavy cruiser. In fact, the only major vessel damaged was the eight-inch gun cruiser *Norfolk*, which was holed underwater. In addition, the depot ship *Iron Duke* received further slight damage from a trio of near misses.

I./KG 30's sole casualty was a 3. *Staffel* machine which lost its bearings during the return flight and crash-landed on an island in the Baltic.

The only Ju 88 not to return safely from the attack on Scapa Flow on 16 March 1940 was this machine, which lost its way and crashed on the Danish island of Laaland. Despite reportedly being an aircraft of 3./KG 30, note the familiar badge on the Junkers' starboard engine nacelle

Unfortunately, the island happened to be Danish and the crew were interned. Their enforced stay in Denmark would not last long, however, for the emphasis of the air war over the North Sea was about to shift dramatically from west to east, as the Wehrmacht prepared to launch Operation *Weserübung* – the invasion of Norway.

Just prior to the start of the Scandinavian campaign, a second *Gruppe* of KG 30 had briefly entered the fray over the 'wet triangle'. The operational debut of II./KG 30 late in March was far from auspicious,

Apart from the single loss, the 16 March raid on Scapa Flow was regarded as a great success. In keeping with the practice of the times, the participating aircrews held a post-mission press conference. Hauptmann Dönch, seated at left below the map of the anchorage, seems content to leave the floor to Oberleutnant Magnussen

for in the space of less than a week, *Gruppenkommandeur* Hauptmann Claus Hinkelbein lost all three of his *Staffelkapitäne*.

The first casualty was Oberleutnant Rudolf Quadt, *Staffelkapitän* of 6./KG 30, who fell victim to anti-aircraft fire while attacking a small coastal convoy off Northumberland on 29 March. Four days later, following another evening raid on Scapa Flow, 4. *Staffel's* Hauptmann Fritz Koch crashed in bad weather over mainland Germany. Twenty-four hours later still, on 3 April, the *Staffelkapitän* of 5./KG 30, Oberleutnant Karl Overweg, was shot down by a Sunderland flying-boat escorting one of the regular North Sea convoys bound for Bergen, in Norway.

It was to disrupt trade-routes such as this, and to eradicate British influence in Scandinavia – but even more to safeguard his own supplies of vital iron ore from Sweden, which was shipped to the Reich through Norwegian waters – which decided Hitler to mount *Weserübung*.

NORWAY

10. *Flieger-Division*, the embryonic air command activated upon the commencement of hostilities with Great Britain to wage anti-shipping in the North Sea, has been upgraded to *Korps* level after only a month in being. Now, as the greatly reinforced X. *Fliegerkorps*, and still

commanded by Generalleutnant Geisler, it controlled all Luftwaffe units – well over 1000 aircraft, including a substantial transport force – assembled for the forthcoming invasion of Norway.

Unlike the bulk of the *Korps'* offensive strength, which was scheduled to cross the Skagerrak and occupy Norway's southern airfields on, or shortly after, W-Day (*Weserübung's* equivalent of the better known D-Day), the three *Gruppen* of Oberstleutnant Loebel's KG 30 would initially remain at Westerland.

It was anticipated that British air and sea forces would react swiftly to the Wehrmacht's move against Norway. As X. *Fliegerkorps'* acknowledged 'anti-shipping experts', KG 30's Ju 88s were therefore to be held at readiness on Sylt to counter any threat posed by surface vessels from across the North Sea. Incidentally, Westerland also housed Z./KG 30, a semi-autonomous *Staffel* equipped with the first examples of the Ju 88C, the heavy-fighter variant of the basic Ju 88A bomber. Although employed primarily in the long-range *Zerstörer* role in the weeks ahead, Z./KG 30 did occasionally operate in conjunction with the bombers of the three main *Gruppen*. At the close of the Norwegian campaign, all connections with the parent *Geschwader* were severed when Z./KG 30 was integrated into the nightfighter arm as 4./NJG 1.

As predicted, when news of Germany's assault on Norway in the early hours of 9 April 1940 became known, the British reaction was immediate. Vessels of the Home Fleet, already at sea and heading north, reversed course southwards towards Stavanger, and the heavy units of the Kriegsmarine reported to be in that area. It was against just such an eventuality that KG 30 had been kept in reserve.

All 47 of the three *Gruppen's* Ju 88s lifted off from Westerland during the mid-afternoon of 9 April. After an hour's flying the first of them sighted the British ships southwest of Bergen. In the action that followed, described as the 'largest air-sea engagement of the war fought to date', the Junkers claimed direct hits on two cruisers. The 9100-ton *Southampton* and the smaller *Galatea* both suffered damage, as too did the destroyer *Gurkha*, which was so severely hit that it foundered some four hours later.

By that time the second wave of Ju 88s, accompanied by Heinkels of KG 26, had also attacked the fleet. Their claims included hits on a battleship and a heavy cruiser. And again they were not far off the mark. The battleship *Rodney* was struck by a bomb, which failed to penetrate her six-inch (150 mm) armoured deck, and near misses damaged the heavy cruiser *Devonshire* as well as both the *Glasgow* and *Sheffield*.

Although devoid of air cover, the ship's anti-aircraft gunners put up a spirited defence, bringing down four of the Ju 88s, including that

The angular, predatory silhouette of the Ju 88 became all too familiar to the crews of the Allied ships, both naval and merchant, supporting the ground forces during the ill-fated Norwegian campaign

The crew of a Ju 88A-1 check their map before the next mission. All are wearing lightweight zippered flying suits, and two have even taken the precaution of already putting on their parachute harnesses

flown by Hauptmann Siegfried Mahrenholtz, the *Gruppenkommandeur* of III./KG 30.

Early the following evening nineteen Ju 88s of I. and II. *Gruppen* again took off from Westerland and set course north-westwards. This time, however, they were not after the ships of the Home Fleet still at large in the North Sea. Their objective was the fleet's oil and fuel depots back at Scapa Flow. Attacking at dusk, two more Junkers would be lost to British anti-aircraft fire.

Next day, 11 April, elements of the *Geschwader* began to transfer in to southern Norway. For the next week they flew a series of armed reconnaissance sweeps as the main emphasis of the ground campaign slowly moved northwards. Nor was air activity over the North Sea all one way. The RAF was playing an increasing role in the fight for Norway, and a number of bombing raids had already been carried out on airfields occupied by the Luftwaffe.

On 17 April a new dimension was introduced when Stavanger-Sola was subjected to a lengthy pre-dawn bombardment from the eight-inch guns of the cruiser *Suffolk*. Although the *vessel*, and her destroyer escort, withdrew before first light, they did not escape retaliation. First to find the tiny force were Heinkels of I./KG 26, which had taken off from Sola itself to chase their recent tormentors. Their two reported hits on the *Suffolk* appear to have had very little effect.

The real damage was inflicted later by Ju 88s of II./KG 30 arriving from Westerland. They intercepted the fleeing ships some 60 miles (96 km) off the Norwegian coast. The cruiser may well have been sunk by the carefully orchestrated attacks launched by the dozen Junkers, had it not been for the sudden appearance of an equal number of RAF Blenheims on a mission from their temporary base at Lossiemouth, in Scotland.

A quartet of Ju 88s display the machine's excellent dive capabilities. In all probability this is a posed picture staged for the benefit of the photographer. In action, rather than following each other down in this manner, pilots would more often than not attack from all points of the compass to confuse and throw off the aim of enemy anti-aircraft gunners

Some aircraft were inevitably hit all the same, although the experience doesn't seem to have dampened the spirits of this cheerful young Feldwebel

The latter's aggressive diving pass broke up the German formation. But the British machines were not long-range fighters – they were a squadron of bombers which happened to be en route to attack Stavanger-Sola in a follow-up to the earlier naval bombardment. Their intervention was purely fortuitous – an instinctive reaction on the part of their leader when he saw the warships' plight. And after a few chaotic minutes all three parties involved in this chance encounter continued on their separate ways. The Junkers of II./KG 30 returned to Westerland and No 107 Sqn's Blenheims resumed course for Sola to deliver their high-level bombing raid as briefed, while the *Suffolk* limped back to Scapa, where she arrived on 18 April with her quarter-deck awash.

By this stage of the campaign Anglo-French ground forces were landing at key points on the coast of central Norway, most notably at Aandalsnes and Namsos, to either side of Trondheim. Norway's third largest town, Trondheim, together with Narvik – far to the north and the departure port for Swedish iron ore shipments to the Reich – had both been taken by the invaders on W-Day. It was over these two isolated German enclaves, which the Allies sought desperately to recapture, that the Ju 88s of KG 30 would operate during the remainder of their participation in the conquest of Norway.

On 18 April bad weather hampered an armed reconnaissance of Namsos by aircraft of I. *Gruppe*, but 24 hours later they spotted a French convoy bringing in reinforcements. A *Kette* of Ju 88s attacked one of the two escorting cruisers, the *Emile Bertin*, damaging her so badly that she was forced to retire to Scapa. On 21 April II./KG 30 scored a more modest success by sinking a pair of anti-submarine trawlers at Aandalsnes.

That same 21 April witnessed the operational appearance of a second Ju 88 unit. For almost the first eight months of the war KG 30 had effectively been the sole *Geschwader* flying the *Wunderbomber* against the foe. During that time, however, several other units had begun converting as the trickle of new Junkers twins coming off the production lines slowly began to increase.

Among the first to commence re-equipment had been *Lehrgeschwader* 1. As its name implies (*Lehr* meaning something akin to 'instructional'), LG 1 was originally established to evaluate, and evolve, operating procedures for the new generation of machines entering Luftwaffe service in the late 'thirties. Each of its component *Gruppen* had thus initially been equipped with a different type of aircraft; e.g. fighter, bomber, dive-bomber, etc. But the gradual conversion to the Ju 88, begun early in 1940, was the start of a process of standardisation which would see the unit emerge as an orthodox – and highly successful – bomber *Geschwader*.

By April 1940 this re-equipment programme was far from complete. III./LG 1 was still flying a mix of

This newly-delivered Ju 88A-5 appears to have aroused a mixture of interest and apathy among the assembled groundcrew at LG 1 . . .

He 111s and Ju 88s when it was transferred to Norway to participate in the latter stages of the campaign. One of the *Gruppe's* first operations – carried out on 21 April – was aimed at ground targets along the railway line linking Trondheim with the south of the country.

Forty-eight hours later a combined force of some two-dozen Junkers from both KG 30 and III./LG 1 returned to the Aandalsnes area to attack shipping in the fjords. Although they claimed the sinking of a small Norwegian steamer, anti-aircraft fire accounted for one of the LG 1 machines.

25 April was a day of considerable activity. In the early afternoon the Ju 88s of III./LG 1 joined forces with the *Lehrgeschwader's* Heinkels to bomb the frozen Lake Lesjaskog – some 30 miles (48 km) inland from Aandalsnes – which was being used as a makeshift landing ground by British fighters. A later sortie saw a similar mixed formation attacking Allied shipping in the fjords on the seaward side of the town. Here, III./LG 1 lost a second Junkers, reportedly shot down by a long-range Blenheim fighter from No 254 Sqn. Much of I./KG 30's attention was also centred on the same area, the sole exception being a single *Kette* despatched – unsuccessfully – against the battleship *Warspite* reported 50 miles (80 km) off the coast.

Over the next few days the Ju 88s of KG 30 and III./LG 1 sank several small Norwegian vessels. The position of the Allied troops to the north and south of Trondheim was by now becoming untenable. Unable to recapture the town in a co-ordinated pincer movement as planned, and suffering continual harassment from the Luftwaffe, the decision was taken to 're-embark the forces landed at Namsos and Aandalsnes as soon as possible'.

The evacuation of Aandalsnes was completed by 1 May. Ju 88s of II./KG 30 attacked one of the Royal Navy cruiser squadrons screening the departing convoys on that date, but without success. Namsos would be cleared two days later. By that time, however, the Junkers of KG 30 and III./LG 1 – together with many of the Heinkel *Gruppen* involved in the

. . . but when aircraft '38' ('L1+MK') later ended her take-off run by digging her wheels and nose into the soft ground, a crowd of spectators soon gathered. Close scrutiny will reveal the open ventral hatch (below the unit's 'Griffon' badge) where the crew made a hasty exit between those external fuel tanks – or are they 500-kg aerial mines!

campaign – had been recalled from Norway to prepare for the forthcoming invasion of France and the Low Countries.

As a postscript to the part played by the Ju 88 in the conquest of Norway, and for the sake of continuity, it is perhaps relevant to mention here that a detachment from II./KG 30 returned to the region a little over a fortnight later (at the height of the *Blitzkrieg* in the west!) to participate in the final act of the Norwegian drama – the battle for Narvik.

On 16 May, when the Junkers attempted to dive-bomb British warships supporting the ground fighting for the town, Fleet Air Arm Skuas from 803 Naval Air Squadron, embarked on *Ark Royal,* shot down two 6. *Staffel* machines. But despite their losses, the Luftwaffe's role at Narvik, as throughout the campaign, would prove decisive. The Ju 88s were in the air daily, attacking targets on land and afloat. The last Allied toehold in Scandinavia could not be held, and in the five days leading up to 8 June 25,000 men were evacuated. The last convoy to leave was escorted by the *Ark Royal.*

During the afternoon of 9 June a *Kette* of 6./KG 30 machines found this group of ships well out to sea. Concentrating on the carrier, all three pilots made dive-bombing attacks, but without result. Like Carl Francke before them, they too had failed to sink the *Ark* . . . albeit far less publicly.

FRANCE AND THE LOW COUNTRIES

The Norwegian campaign has since been described as a 'pre-emptive sideshow'. Although this is an over-simplification, it is undeniably true that the Führer's eyes were fixed firmly on the west, and the old enemy; France.

The winter months of 1939-40 – the period of the so-called 'Phoney War' – had witnessed a rapid expansion in the ranks of the Luftwaffe. But the increase in strength, and introduction of new types, had not been evenly spread. The numbers of Ju 88s delivered to frontline units still fell far short of the 'mighty fleet' which had been demanded by Göring a year before hostilities had commenced.

When KG 30 and LG 1 returned to Germany at the beginning of May 1940, they constituted by far the greatest concentration of Junkers bombers on the western front (even though only one *Gruppe* of the latter unit had as yet converted fully from its earlier Heinkels). Alongside them as part of *Luftflotte* 2 on the northern flank of the coming offensive (but subordinated to a different *Fliegerkorps*), III./KG 4 had still to complete its re-equipment with the Ju 88.

Lfl. 2's force of six Ju 88 *Kampfgruppen* (four fully, two partially equipped, for a total of some 100+ serviceable machines in all) was nonetheless five times the size of that deployed by neighbouring *Luftflotte* 3 in southern Germany.

A new emblem joins the ranks of Ju 88 units – the famous 'Edelweiss' of KG 51

Arguably the most famous Ju 88 pilot of them all, Oberleutnant Werner Baumbach is pictured here being presented with the Knight's Cross, awarded for his outstanding performance during the Norwegian campaign. Further spectacular anti-shipping successes would see the Oak Leaves added in 1941 and the Swords in 1942. Like Storp, Oberleutnant Baumbach was another early wartime bomber ace who subsequently rose to the position of *General der Kampflieger*. By war's end he was commanding KG 200

There, only one *Gruppe*, II./KG 51, was fully operational on the Ju 88. At the start of the campaign in the west, I./KG 51 was still in the throes of conversion from the He 111 and, together the two *Gruppen*, would contribute just 22 serviceable aircraft to the opening rounds of the battle for France.

It is, perhaps, worth pointing out that the first reconnaissance versions of the Ju 88 were also entering service at this time, proving yet again, like the RAF's later Mosquito, the Junkers' basic design was highly adaptable and well suited for a variety of roles. All but two of the ten long-range reconnaissance *Staffeln* divided between *Luftflotten* 2 and 3 on the western front now operated two or three new Ju 88s alongside their standard Heinkels or Dorniers.

The *Blitzkrieg* against France and the Low Countries was launched in the early hours of 10 May 1940. As in Poland the previous autumn, the first objective in this new 'lightning war' was to neutralise the enemy's air power. On the northern flank of the invading armies, the Ju 88 *Kampfgruppen* of *Luftflotte* 2 were therefore to employ their proven dive-bombing abilities, but not against shipping. Instead, they were to perform pin-point attacks on the anti-aircraft defences protecting Dutch and Belgian airfields.

One of the pilots of II./KG 30, based at Oldenburg, was a 23-year old Oberleutnant who would duly rise to the position of *General der Kampfflieger* – Werner Baumbach;

While it was the Storps and Baumbachs who grabbed the headlines and gained the glory, it was those unsung heroes, the groundcrews, who kept the bombers flying. For the mechanics ('Black men' in Luftwaffe parlance, which was a reference to the colour of their work overalls) no job was too big – be it changing a complete engine . . .

'Our sudden transfer from Norway back to an airfield in north-west Germany, and the reports appearing in the press of English preparations for landings in Holland and Belgium, gave us a fair clue of what was about to happen.

'During the night of 9-10 May the decision was taken. We received orders to attack and destroy flak emplacements around airfields in the Rotterdam-Hague-Delft areas. Our preparations were carried out under the cover of darkness. For the first time in a long while our aircraft were being loaded with bombs of a smaller calibre. The armourers and ground-crews worked feverishly, while the flyers tried to grab a few hours sleep.

'Take-off was scheduled for 0430 hours.

'It was the same familiar routine which we knew all too well from our recent night operations against Scapa Flow and Narvik. A final short briefing a few minutes before take-off. Each individual aircraft commander is given a specific target. The *Staffelkapitän* reads out the latest situation report. Watches are synchronised. And moments later the trucks arrive to take the crews out to their aircraft.

'The air vibrates with the roar of the engines. Searchlights are switched on momentarily. carving a narrow corridor through the pitch black night. The signal is given. The *Gruppenkommandeur* releases his brakes. As his machine starts to roll, others quickly jockey into position in his wake.

'We lift off – a quick glance at the clock on the instrument panel reveals that it is exactly 0431 hours.

'I can just make out the *Kette* ahead of me. We fly in close formation. The flames from our exhausts help us keep station. As we slowly climb to our given altitude, it gets lighter minute by minute. One *Staffel* after another rises out of the gloom. Far below us ground mist shrouds the Emsland moors.

'Then we are over Holland – enemy territory. My navigator takes a few readings and announces, "We're exactly on course". I have switched on the autopilot. We fortify ourselves by demolishing a packet of biscuits. On my left N's *Staffel* slowly slides up alongside us.

'We fly over several Dutch towns. A sprinkling of flak, but it's far below and we take no notice. The ground fog has cleared a little, but we ourselves are flying through a thick layer of mist. The contours of the Dutch landscape unrolling beneath our wings are indistinct.

'Soon we reach our target area. Bursts of heavy flak ahead of us. We still can't see 'our' airfield. The mist is too thick. But it's also our saviour, for just at that moment my rear-gunner shouts a warning, "Enemy fighters to the left and below – twin booms!" I recognise them – Dutch Koolhoven machines. I make a wide turn to the right and sink into the mist – my two wingmen following.

'We have got our bearings now and should soon be over the target. Ahead of us the first *Ketten* begin to peel off ready to start their dives. And there in front of us, just off to one side, we suddenly see "our" airfield. The flak grows heavier. The field is ringed by a continuous ripple of fire as the batteries send up a barrage which explodes and hangs in the air above the airfield like a thick grey carpet.

'The wireless-operator's shout of "Fighters!" distracts me from our target for a moment. But then I hear through the headphones, "They're ours!" The Me 109s and Me 110s have rendezvoused with us precisely on

schedule, and are guarding the airspace above us. The bomb-aimer checks his switches. "All clear", he reports. The little red light glows in front of me. My thumb hovers over the bomb-release button.

'We commence the attack. I signal my two wingmen. Our formation breaks apart as each seeks the best position to start his dive within our limited target area. The order of the day is approach together, attack singly.

'My bomb-aimer and I both have our eyes fixed firmly on our own objective – a flak emplacement in the middle of what appears to be a large farmyard. It is on slightly raised ground and dominates the surrounding region. We have to destroy it, otherwise the paratroops following us in will be put at great risk.

'The first bombs are already exploding on the southern edge of the airfield. I decide to attack from the north to make full use of the element of surprise. I approach in a steep glide and then tip the nose forward. The farmyard rushes up to meet me, firmly centred in my sights. I release the bombs. Our front gunners hammer into the flak position as we pull out at low level. "A direct hit!" the rear gunner reports.

'Banking away, we watch the farm buildings collapse like a house of cards. The guns are silent. "The grass won't grow there any more", Thies remarks in his usual dry manner.

'We set course for home. I just have time to say, "Keep a sharp lookout for enemy fighters!" when we are attacked out of the morning sun by a Lockheed Hudson. The gunners let fly with everything they have got,

. . . or too small – and judging from the size of the tool box being carried here from the mobile workshop to the waiting Ju 88, they didn't come much smaller than this!

28

while I search anxiously for a protective cloud – nothing! Our only hope is to stand the crate on its head and get down close to the ground. The enemy *Zerstörer* is almost on top of us. I can clearly see the Dutch markings.

'Still firing from all barrels, we manage to get away. The *Zerstörer* gives up the chase. And we quickly realise why – he has been bounced by one of our own Me 110s. At the same instant we spot the first parachutists and the leading wave of Ju 52s bringing in the airborne troops.

'During our flight home we can see our ground columns flooding down the straight roads of Holland. The German advance in the west has begun.'

Written shortly after the events described, Baumbach's account reveals a certain deficiency in enemy aircraft recognition! The twin-boomed 'Koolhovens' were obviously Fokker G.Is, and although Baumbach may well have been familiar with the portly profile of the Lockheed Hudson from recent encounters with Coastal Command aircraft of that type over Norway, there were none then serving with the Dutch air force. In all likelihood, the Junkers' assailant had been one of the twin-engined, twin-tailed Fokker T.V bombers which had taken to the air to escape the Luftwaffe's co-ordinated raids on the Dutch airfields.

Mechanics work on the port engine of another machine from LG 1 which is already bombed up ready for its next mission – could the problem have anything to do with whatever happened to that spinner?

29

The Junkers had done their job well, for both the Dutch and Belgian air forces had been hit hard in this first day of all-out war in the west. But the Ju 88s *Gruppen* had not escaped unscathed. Although Baumbach's unit lost only one aircraft – a 5. *Staffel* machine over Waalhaven – four machines from I./KG 30 failed to return. Another four of the newly-equipped 9./KG 4 were shot down (three reportedly by Dutch fighters) over Schiphol. And of those attacking targets in Belgium, two III./KG 30 machines fell victim to anti-aircraft fire near Charleroi. A third, of III./LG 1 – initially believed also to have succumbed to ground defences at Wevelghem – may have been the 8. *Staffel* aircraft claimed by RAF Hurricanes which crashed near Mons.

The dozen casualties suffered by the Ju 88s on 10 May would be their heaviest single day's losses of the entire campaign. On 11 May all aircraft returned safely from further strikes against targets in the Low Countries. But 24 hours later there were several encounters between the Junkers and UK-based RAF fighters (including two-seater Defiants) off the Dutch coast. Although sources differ as to the exact details, it would appear that two KG 30 machines were lost, with one falling to the fighters, the other to naval anti-aircraft fire – while an aircraft of III./LG 1 escaped with minor damage.

Seen on a captured French airbase, 3./KG 51's *'Emil-Ludwig'* survived the French campaign, but would be one of the ten 'Edelweiss' aircraft which failed to return from a raid on the Portsmouth area on 12 August 1940

A KG 51 aircraft comes home to roost, sinking gently towards its lengthening shadow after another hard day's campaigning over France

Late on 14 May the Dutch began negotiating for a surrender. By that time the Ju 88 *Gruppen* had turned their attention on northern Belgium, supporting the advance of the ground troops and attacking coastal targets. It was at this juncture, too, that II./KG 30 was pulled out of the campaign. While the experienced crews of the reinforced 6. *Staffel* returned to Norway and the fighting around Narvik, the remainder of the *Gruppe* withdrew to its peace-time station, Perleberg, to carry out a concentrated training programme for its new members. This lasted the best part of a month, and culminated in dummy dive-bombing attacks on the old World War 1 battleship *Hessen*, now reconstructed and serving in the Baltic as a radio-controlled target-ship.

Far removed from the activities of the majority of the Ju 88 *Gruppen* on the northern flank, as the sole unit operating the Junkers bomber under *Luftflotte* 3 in the south, KG 51 had been covering the main thrust of the German offensive through the Ardennes and deep into France. Their primary targets were French lines of communications behind the fighting front.

They had already flown the first of such missions, and suffered their first casualties, when Hermann Göring phoned the *Geschwaderkommodore* of KG 51, Oberst Josef Kammhuber (he of later nightfighting fame), exhorting them to even greater efforts. The target for 16 May was to be the French rail network south of Nancy. The Generalfeldmarschall then turned the screw even tighter, stressing that he was expecting great things from Kammhuber's KG 51, equipped as it now was with the new Ju 88 dive-bomber.

Despite a shaky start – a rendezvous and long approach flight in seven-tenths cloud proving something of an ordeal for crews not yet fully trained in blind-flying the Junkers – the objectives were attacked successfully and without loss. But Kammhuber himself had a narrow

It seems here as if congratulations are being offered on yet one more mission successfully completed. But a closer examination of the photograph reveals the jettisoned cockpit canopy on the ground behind the two crew members, plus the fact that this KG 51 machine has completely shed its mainwheel tyres and is resting on its hubs – obviously this was a hairier landing than at first appears to have been the case

Although of dubious quality, this wartime press picture nonetheless does genuinely appear to show a Ju 88 (of KG 51) committed to an almost vertical dive – note the air-brake extended beneath the port wing

escape on the return flight. The cloud had thickened and the wind was gusting strongly when his autopilot suddenly disengaged. The Junkers immediately tipped over and plunged earthwards. Wrestling with the controls, watching the altimeter unwinding 'like a spinning top' and noting, with almost clinical detachment, the needle of the ASI jammed against the stop at 720 km/h (447 mph) – 160 km/h (100 mph) above the normal dive speed – Kammhuber thought his time had come.

Somehow, he managed to pull the Ju 88 out of its screaming dive just as it broke through the low-lying cloud base. By some miracle they were flying along a deep valley. To either side of them the crew could see steep, tree-covered hillsides, lashed by rain, their tops hidden in scudding cloud. Gingerly, Kammhuber threaded his way back to Lechfeld, where the sight of the Ju 88 was greeted with disbelief – the normally smooth surface of its wings was one huge mass of wrinkles. Kammhuber's involuntary dive had not only underlined the inherent strength of the Junkers' airframe – the wings of any comparable machine would have been ripped completely off – it had also helped iron out another 'bug'. Future Ju 88s would be fitted with more efficient autopilots.

But an airframe, however strong, is not proof against well-aimed .303-in machine-gun fire, and did little to protect the three KG 51 aircraft which were shot down by AASF Hurricanes during the sprawling series of clashes between Soissons and Reims three days later.

Meanwhile, *Luftflotte* 2's Ju 88s continued their offensive along the coastal belt, attacking not only Belgian, but now French channel ports too. This brought them within even closer range of RAF Fighter Command, and both KG 30 and LG 1 suffered casualties as they bombed the harbour installations at Ostend, Calais and Boulogne. But it was the fourth port along that same short stretch of coast which would become the focus of considerable Luftwaffe attention for the next two weeks – Dunkirk.

Despite the near constant aerial bombardment of the harbour itself, the nearby beaches and offshore shipping, some third-of-a-million men succeeded in escaping across the Channel to England. But there had been one among that multitude who was anxious to escape in the opposite direction – inland.

It had all begun on 29 May when Ju 88s of KG 30 were making yet another attack on the evacuation ships standing off the beaches. Oberleutnant von Oelhaven had just selected a 3000-tonner as his target when an anti-aircraft shell struck his port engine. Streaming smoke, the Ju 88 became separated from the rest of the formation and was pounced upon by RAF fighters. With its rudder controls now shot away, the Junkers began to go down in a wide left-hand turn.

Von Oelhaven had to abandon all hopes of reaching friendly territory. He opted instead to put the damaged Junkers down in the sea some 25 yards off the beach at Nieuport. The navigator had jettisoned the canopy at the last moment and the crew managed to scramble clear and get under cover before enemy troops arrived to investigate. But the only part of the Ju 88 visible above water was the tip of its aerial mast and they soon lost interest.

A I./KG 30 crew clamber gratefully out of their flying suits. Two points of interest here: firstly, although reportedly photographed in the early summer of 1940, this Ju 88 has been given temporary night-camouflaged undersides (on the original print a swastika can be seen scratched the wrong way round in the black distemper below the exhaust stubs!). Secondly, the aircraft carries the combination markings of a 'Diving Eagle' *Gruppe* badge on the nose and 'Chamberlain's Umbrella' on the engine nacelle

The crew decided to split into pairs and seek separate hiding places to await the arrival of the German army. Von Oelhaven and his Feldwebel gunner were later discovered in the cellar of a ruined house in Nieuport and marched along the coast to the evacuation beaches nearer Dunkirk. There, makeshift landing stages had been constructed by driving trucks into the water and laying planks across them.

Von Oelhaven was being escorted along one of these precarious crowded walkways to be taken to England when another bombing raid began. Seizing his chance in the resulting confusion, the Oberleutnant jumped into the water and quickly ducked beneath one of the trucks.

There he stayed for the next 36 hours, oily water coming up to his chin at every high tide, listening to the constant shuffling of feet only inches above his head. When he finally emerged, the beaches were much quieter. Grabbing an army greatcoat and tin hat from the piles of abandoned British equipment strewn around, von Oelhaven sought shelter in one of the hastily dug holes that pockmarked the dunes behind the beach. He was ravenously hungry, but that posed no problem. The BEF had also divested itself of most of its rations. Tins of bully-beef, the *Engländer's* staple fare, lay scattered in the dunes like 'patches of bright red flowers'.

Declining the invitation of several small groups of French rear-guard troops to join them in their trek into Dunkirk town to await captivity, von Oelhaven stayed put. His four-day odyssey was finally brought to an end by the appearance of two German infantrymen cautiously advancing through the dunes. Just what this pair made of the figure running excitedly towards them, struggling out of a British greatcoat to reveal the oil and salt-stained Luftwaffe uniform beneath, is not on record. But as his

Little doubt about the time of year when this photograph was taken, for the heat of the sun is almost tangible. Perhaps it's the protective cover on the wheel of this bombed-up A-5 of LG 1 – or is it the state of undress of the character on the right?

fellow pilots remarked, with a name like his – meaning literally 'of the oil harbour' – it just couldn't have happened to anyone else!

The evacuation of Allied forces from Dunkirk brought to an end the first phase of the *Blitzkrieg* in the west. But it was still necessary to defeat the bulk of the French army massed beyond the Somme. Although the element of surprise was no longer present, the Luftwaffe opened this second stage of the offensive in their customary manner – by striking at the enemy's air bases.

In fact, Operation *Paula*, launched on 3 June, was even broader in scope. Its aim was to knock out not just the French airfields, but also aircraft manufacturing plants and other industrial complexes in the greater Paris area. As part of the attacking force, KG 4's assigned objective was Le Bourget. For the first time their aircraft would be dropping *Flamm* C 250 incendiary bombs. These oil-filled missiles – and others like them, soon to be scattered in their thousands on Britain's towns and cities – were then still so new that their ballistic details had to be phoned through from the Rechlin test centre only moments before take-off.

After *Paula*, Luftwaffe bombing raids continued unabated as the French withdrew south and westwards, falling back from one river line to the next. On 5 June three Ju 88s of III./LG 1 failed to return from operations over the Seine around Rouen. Further south, III./KG 4 was also to lose several Junkers to anti-aircraft fire while harassing Allied troops retreating along the valley of the Loire between Orléans and Tours.

III./KG 4's last Ju 88 casualties of the campaign occurred on 15 June. This was also the day which saw II./KG 30's return to the west after their long sojourn in the Homeland. The time spent perfecting their dive-bombing techniques against the ancient *Hessen* in the Baltic was to be put to immediate use, for they were to attack shipping and dockside installations at Cherbourg.

Taking off from their new base at Le Culot, in Belgium, the Junkers of the 'Eagle' *Geschwader* landed to refuel at Amiens, before crossing out over the Channel coast at Le Havre and making a wide sweep in order to approach their target from the seaward side. The tactic obviously paid off, for all aircraft returned safely from this raid on France's most important

Another LG 1 Ju 88A-5, this time seen on the compass platform of a permanent base 'somewhere in Germany' (the *Geschwader's* jumping-off point for the *Blitzkrieg* in the west was Düsseldorf). Such amenities would soon be a thing of the past . . .

naval base. Not so the next day, however, when their second mission was flown against bridges over the confluence of the Rivers Cher and Loire at Tours, where two Ju 88s – both of 5. *Staffel* – fell victim to the French anti-aircraft defences.

The day after that, 17 June, II./KG 30 turned their attention back to shipping – more specifically, to the mass of evacuation craft of all sizes gathered off the port of St Nazaire at the mouth of the Loire.

One of the biggest vessels in the estuary was the 16,243-ton Cunard White Star liner *Lancastria*, now serving as a troopship. Other Ju 88 *Gruppen* were also active over the target area and it is still impossible to state with certainty which unit carried out the co-ordinated dive-bombing attacks which sank her. But sunk she was, in one of the costliest, most inexplicable and hushed up single maritime disasters of the war. Costly, because some half of the 5000 people aboard her – British Army and RAF personnel, and French refugees – were lost. Inexplicable, because they perished on a calm summer's day in a busy roadstead crowded with other ships.

Despite the intense anti-aircraft fire and the presence of French Morane fighters, all of II./KG 30's Junkers again returned to base, although one was riddled with more than seventy 7.5 mm bullet holes. With his undercarriage damaged and unable to salvo or jettison his bomb load either electrically or mechanically, Unteroffizier Geffgen pulled off a perfect belly landing using the four 250-kg (550-lb) underwing bombs as landing skids!

On 18 June the Luftwaffe suffered the last two Ju 88 operational losses (out of a total of some 80) incurred during the invasion of the Low Countries and France. One of the two was a 9./LG 1 machine which came down over Brest. The other was an aircraft of I./KG 51. Throughout much of the recent *Blitzkrieg* KG 51 had been in a state of transition, those *Staffeln* which had begun the campaign flying He 111s being rotated piecemeal back to Germany to convert to the Ju 88.

The number of aircraft lost in training accidents by KG 51 added greatly to their overall casualty rate, which was – perhaps not surprisingly – among the highest of all the Ju 88 units currently engaged in the fighting in the west. That fighting was not to last much longer, for Marshall Pétain of France had already announced his appeal for an armistice. On 18 June the first aircraft of I./KG 51 had touched down at Paris-Orly. Two days later the rest of the *Geschwader* joined them on other airfields close to Paris. The aircrew quickly took advantage of their proximity to the French capital. But they would have little time to enjoy the company of the dancers from the *Pigalle*, or sample the delights of the topless revue bars of Montmartre.

For as Prime Minister Winston Churchill was declaring defiantly from across the Channel, 'The Battle of France is over. The Battle of Britain is about to begin'.

. . . for as LG 1 moved forward into occupied France, conditions became decidedly more spartan. Here, men of the unit's attached FBK (*Flughafenbetriebskompanie* – airfield servicing company) dig slit trenches in an open meadow which is serving as an advanced landing ground. Unlike the 'black men', who were responsible solely for the maintenance of the aircraft, FBK personnel wore a light-coloured working uniform

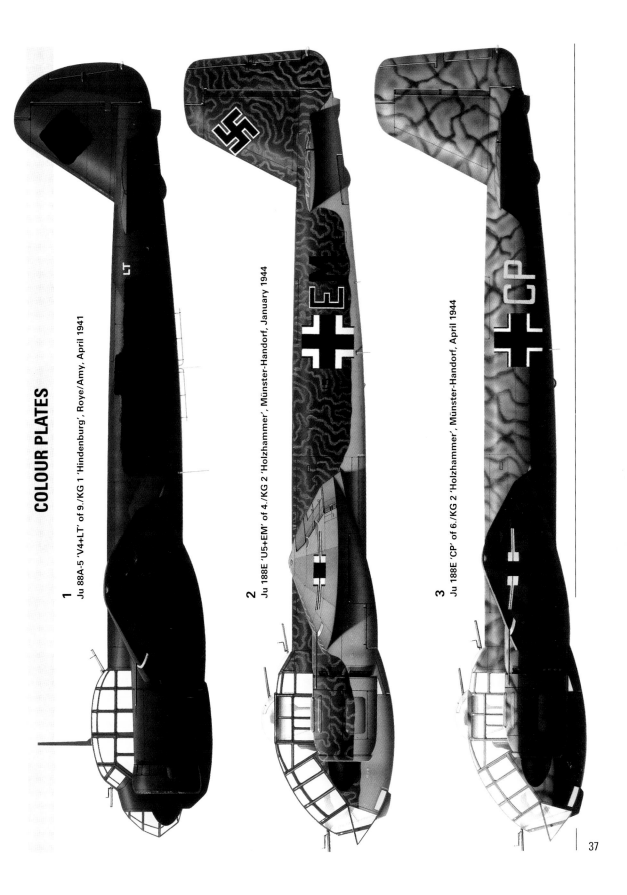

COLOUR PLATES

1
Ju 88A-5 'V4+LT' of 9./KG 1 'Hindenburg', Roye/Amy, April 1941

2
Ju 188E 'U5+EM' of 4./KG 2 'Holzhammer', Münster-Handorf, January 1944

3
Ju 188E 'CP' of 6./KG 2 'Holzhammer', Münster-Handorf, April 1944

4
Ju 88A-1 '5J+CS' of 8./KG 4 'General Wever', Kirchhellen, June 1940

5
Ju 188E '3E+EL' of 3./KG 6, Chievres, October 1943

6
Ju 188A-14 '3E+NS' of 8./KG 6, Melsbroek, February 1944

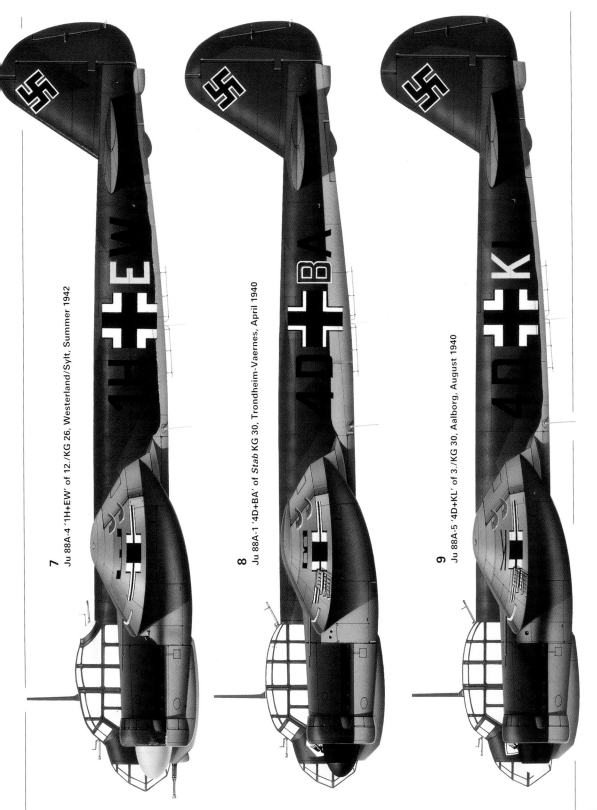

7
Ju 88A-4 '1H+EW' of 12./KG 26, Westerland/Sylt, Summer 1942

8
Ju 88A-1 '4D+BA' of *Stab* KG 30, Trondheim-Vaernes, April 1940

9
Ju 88A-5 '4D+KL' of 3./KG 30, Aalborg, August 1940

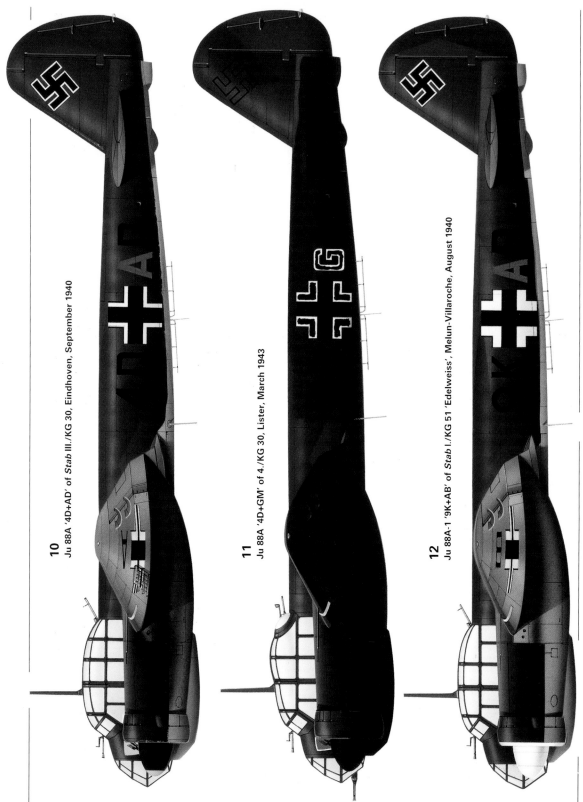

10
Ju 88A '4D+AD' of *Stab* III./KG 30, Eindhoven, September 1940

11
Ju 88A '4D+GM' of 4./KG 30, Lister, March 1943

12
Ju 88A-1 '9K+AB' of *Stab* I./KG 51 'Edelweiss', Melun-Villaroche, August 1940

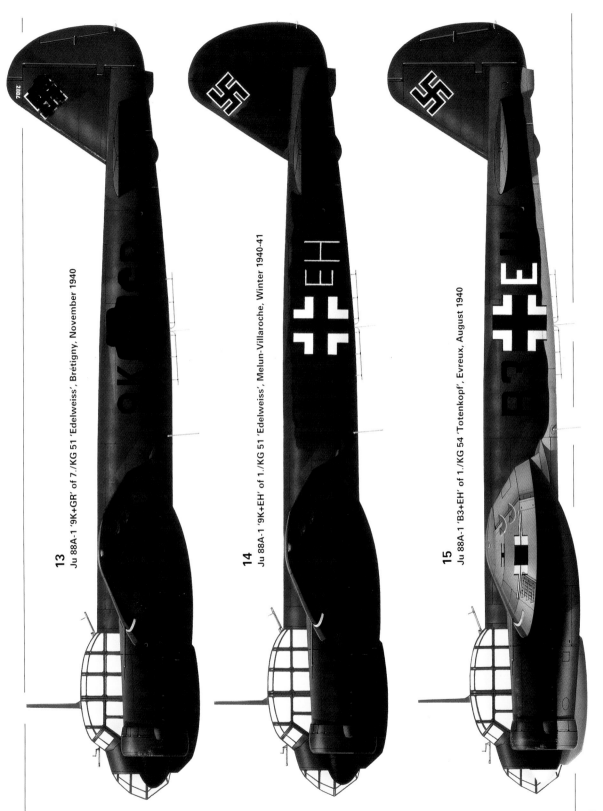

13
Ju 88A-1 '9K+GR' of 7./KG 51 'Edelweiss', Brétigny, November 1940

14
Ju 88A-1 '9K+EH' of 1./KG 51 'Edelweiss', Melun-Villaroche, Winter 1940-41

15
Ju 88A-1 'B3+EH' of 1./KG 54 'Totenkopf', Evreux, August 1940

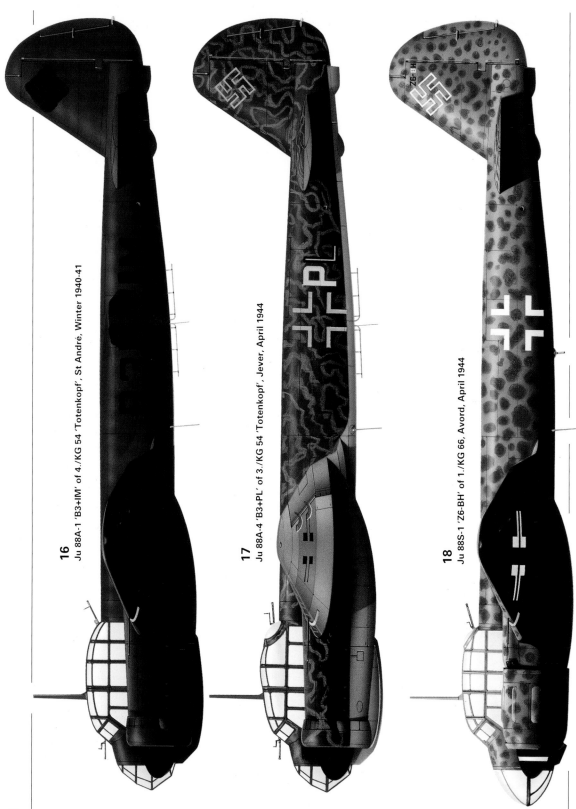

16
Ju 88A-1 'B3+IM' of 4./KG 54 'Totenkopf', St André, Winter 1940-41

17
Ju 88A-4 'B3+PL' of 3./KG 54 'Totenkopf', Jever, April 1944

18
Ju 88S-1 'Z6-BH' of 1./KG 66, Avord, April 1944

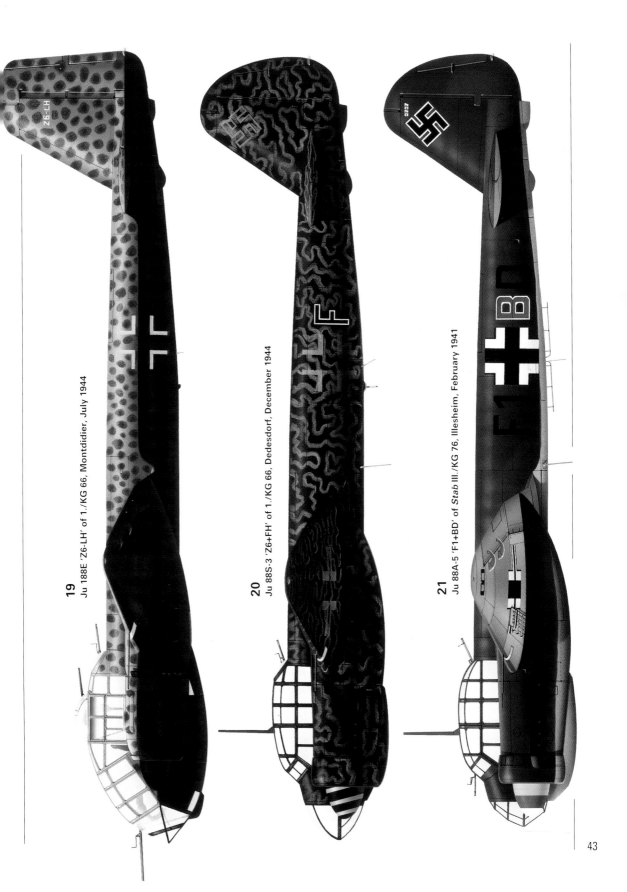

19
Ju 188E 'Z6-LH' of 1./KG 66, Montdidier, July 1944

20
Ju 88S-3 'Z6+FH' of 1./KG 66, Dedesdorf, December 1944

21
Ju 88A-5 'F1+BD' of *Stab* III./KG 76, Illesheim, February 1941

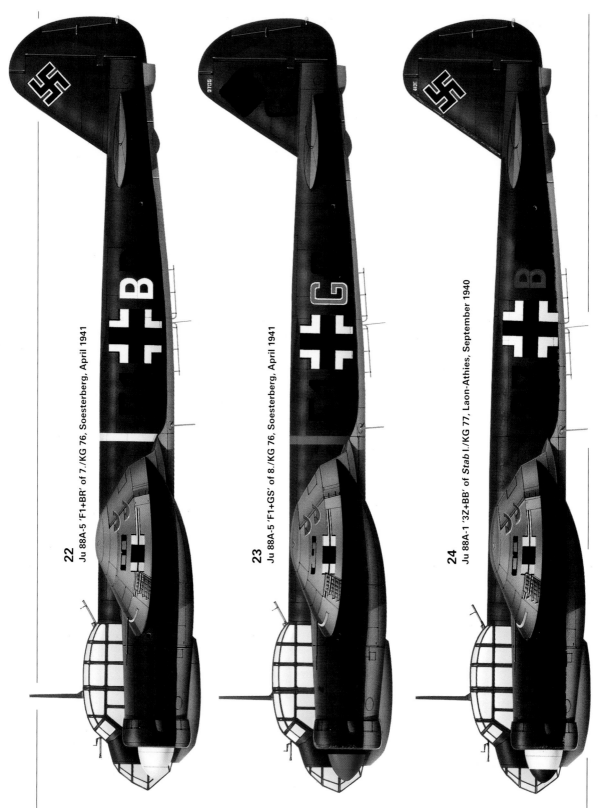

22
Ju 88A-5 'F1+BR' of 7./KG 76, Soesterberg, April 1941

23
Ju 88A-5 'F1+GS' of 8./KG 76, Soesterberg, April 1941

24
Ju 88A-1 '3Z+BB' of Stab I./KG 77, Laon-Athies, September 1940

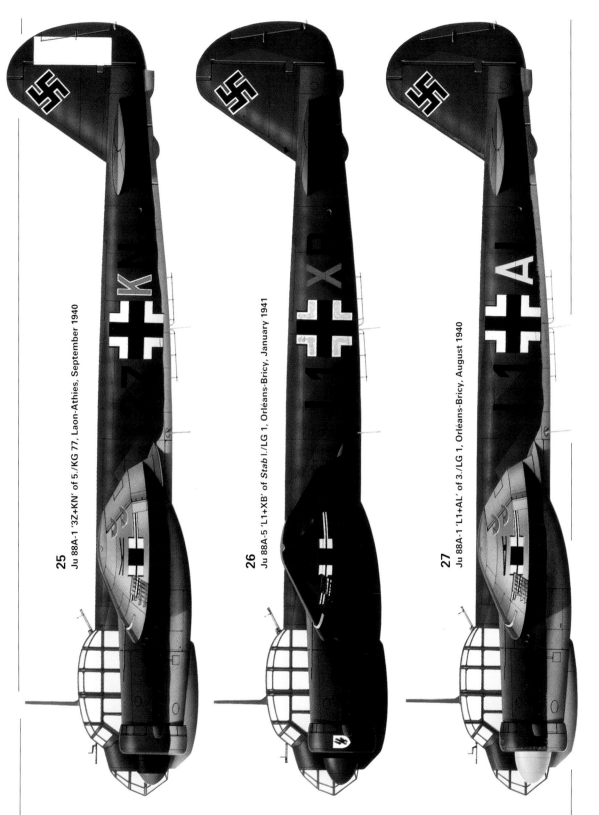

25
Ju 88A-1 '3Z+KN' of 5./KG 77, Laon-Athies, September 1940

26
Ju 88A-5 'L1+XB' of *Stab* I./LG 1, Orléans-Bricy, January 1941

27
Ju 88A-1 'L1+AL' of 3./LG 1, Orléans-Bricy, August 1940

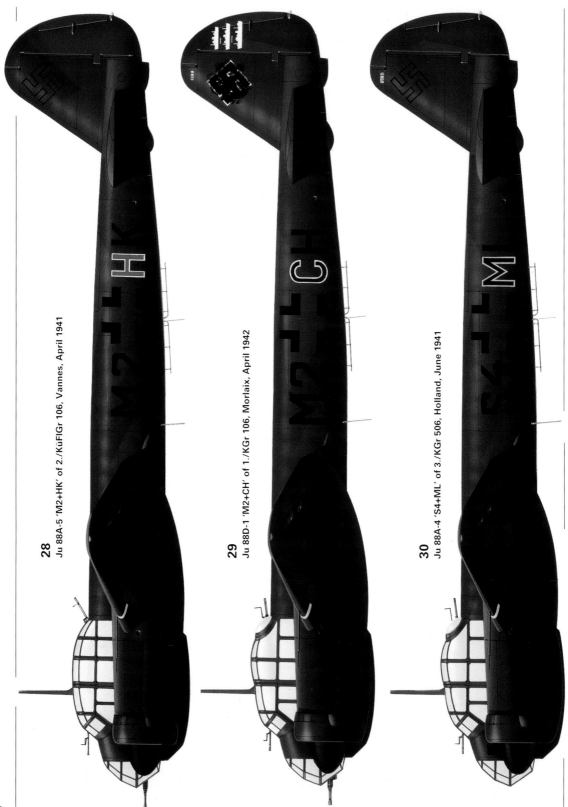

28
Ju 88A-5 'M2+HK' of 2./KüFlGr 106, Vannes, April 1941

29
Ju 88D-1 'M2+CH' of 1./KGr 106, Morlaix, April 1942

30
Ju 88A-4 'S4+ML' of 3./KGr 506, Holland, June 1941

1940-43 – TRIAL BY FIRE

Many German sources quote Sunday 23 June 1940 as the day the Luftwaffe launched its *Luftschlacht um England*. Although this was a full week before 1 July, the somewhat arbitrary date favoured by some British historians as marking the start of the air campaign against the UK, the first raid of any significance had in fact been carried out even earlier.

It was on the night of 18/19 June – only hours after the Ju 88s of I./KG 51 had flown in to Paris-Orly – that a force of some 70 Luftwaffe bombers, including the He 111s of KG 4, crossed the North Sea to attack England's eastern counties.

A few unfortunates thus underwent an almost seamless, if somewhat painful, transition from bombing France to bombing England (five of KG 4's Heinkels failed to return from this first raid). However, for the vast majority of the Luftwaffe units recently engaged against the French there were at least a few days, if not weeks, respite before they turned their attention towards the one remaining enemy.

The Ju 88 *Gruppen* were luckier than many in this respect, for they were not directly involved in the opening round of the projected invasion of England. This was aimed at closing the Channel to British shipping and was a task entrusted primarily to the single-engined Ju 87 dive-bombers (see *Osprey Combat Aircraft 1 - Junkers Ju 87 Stukageschwader 1937-41* for further details).

In the meantime, the Luftwaffe continued to increase its Ju 88 bombing force. The remaining Heinkel crews of III./KG 4 had begun converting to the Junkers the day after the signing of the French Armistice, and the end of the fighting in France also provided the opportunity for KG 51 and I-III. *Gruppen* of LG 1 to re-equip fully with Ju 88s.

Four other *Gruppen* were undergoing similar conversion, including I. and II./KG 54, who had been withdrawn from operations in the immediate aftermath of the Dunkirk evacuation to exchange their surviving He 111s for Junkers. Their losses had been so heavy during the first phase of the *Blitzkrieg* that III./KG 54 had been disbanded to help make good their numbers.

Also re-equipping during June-July was II./KG 76, the first ex-Do 17 *Gruppe* to convert to the Ju 88, and the autonomous *Kampfgruppe*

Several new units were equipped with the Ju 88 at the start of the Battle of Britain, including KG 54 'Totenkopf'. 3. *Staffel's 'Emil-Ludwig'* sports the 'Death's Head' badge which gave the *Geschwader* its name

Fully kitted up in lightweight flying suit and inflatable life-jacket, a pensive Werner Baumbach poses in front of his Ju 88A-4, which appears to be armed with a pair of 500-kg bombs

806. This latter outfit was one of the original naval coastal units (*Küstenfliegergruppen*) which had operated flying-boats in the early weeks of the war before becoming land-based, receiving He 111 bombers, and being redesignated as *Kampfgruppen*. KGr 806, whose commissioned aircrew were still predominantly Kriegsmarine personnel, was the first such *Kampfgruppe* selected for conversion to the Junkers.

But it was the 'Old Guard' in the form of KG 30, over their old stamping grounds along the east coast of Scotland, who were to suffer the first Ju 88 casualties of the Battle of Britain period proper. On 3 July 1940 a trio of 8. *Staffel* machines failed to return to their base in Denmark from an armed reconnaissance of the Aberdeen area. And at least two of the three had fallen prey to old enemies – the Spitfires of No 603 Sqn.

This probing of Britain's coastal towns and defences, from Scotland round to Wales, would remain the Junkers' principal occupation for the remainder of the month. Carried out in small numbers, their losses were commensurately low, but they did include aircraft from two of the new *Gruppen*. On 16 July II./KG 54 suffered its first Ju 88 combat casualty when 6. *Staffel's* 'Gustav-Paula' was shot down by No 601 Sqn Hurricanes off the southern tip of the Isle of Wight. II./KG 76's first operational loss was also the result of a brush with Hurricanes, from No 145 Sqn, off the Sussex coast on 29 July.

One unit which did venture inland during these early weeks was KG 51, and they in turn had to contend with less predictable hazards. Briefed to attack the Gloster aircraft factory at Hucclecote on the afternoon of

En route to attack Gloster's factory at Hucclecote on 25 July 1940, 5./KG 51's '9K+GN' collided with a Miles Master trainer (flown by a Sgt G H Bell) from No 5 Flying Training Squadron close to South Cerney airfield and crashed to earth on this Gloucestershire hillside. All four crew members baled out but only three survived to become PoWs, the fourth falling to his death when his parachute failed to open

25 July, an aircraft of II. *Gruppe* was involved in a mid-air collision with a Miles Master trainer and crashed near Cirencester. Flying an even deeper penetration mission to Crewe in the early hours of 28 July, a I./KG 51 machine lost its bearings, ran out of fuel, and came down in Sussex.

The Junkers' low loss rate was less a reflection on the thinly-stretched nature of the defences, than on the aircraft's own turn of speed and manoeuvrability. Throughout the entire Battle, of the triumvirate of Luftwaffe twin-engined bombers involved, the Ju 88 would continue to suffer far fewer casualties per sortie than either the He 111 or the Do 17. Pilots of RAF Fighter Command also readily conceded that the Junkers was the hardest of the three to bring down, and despite their best efforts, the daily claims for Ju 88s destroyed over Great Britain remained stubbornly low.

On only ten days during the four months from July to October did Ju 88 losses exceed three aircraft. More often than not there was just a single casualty, if any at all. And only on four occasions did the total of Ju 88s

After take-off, the mainwheels of the Ju 88 turned through 90 degrees before retracting to lie flat in the engine nacelles. This pilot has just selected 'gear up' and the starboard wheel is already beginning to swivel

Despite the amount of material published over the years on the subject of Luftwaffe unit badges, some examples still defy identification. This is one such – a runic character, possibly in red, with some indecipherable black writing along its length – sported by a rather sorry-looking Ju 88

Another Ju 88 which has come to grief on returning to base. The splintered port propeller would seem to suggest undercarriage failure, but the crew, apparently unconcerned, are in the process of proving the old adage that 'any landing you can walk away from is a good one'

A late wartime portrait of Oberst Hajo Hermann. Although one of III./KG 30's most successful pilots during the early months of hostilities, flying 320 bombing missions, he is now best remembered as the originator of the 'Wilde Sau' nightfighting concept. Captured in 1945, Hajo Hermann spent more than ten years in Soviet captivity

lost climb into double figures – nearly every time as a result of exceptional circumstances.

It was a sobering fact that, in July, the number of aircraft written off in training accidents, crashes and as a result of malfunctions over mainland Europe exceeded the 20-odd lost to direct enemy action. It could almost have been argued that, once they were masters of their machine, the safest place for a Ju 88 crew to be in the summer of 1940 was on one of their fast, hit-and-run raids over southern England – but try telling that to the *Staffelkapitän* of 7./KG 30, one Hauptmann Hajo Herrmann.

He was leading a mine-laying sortie over Plymouth harbour on the night of 22 July when, in a slow shallow dive, he inadvertently 'pancaked' on top of a barrage balloon! After a few seconds with this bulbous, and highly inflammable, appendage trapped beneath its belly, the Ju 88 fell off upside down. Herrmann jettisoned the canopy roof and was about to order his crew to bale out when he managed to regain control of the machine low over the water.

Releasing his mines and bracketed by anti-aircraft fire, Herrmann raced out over Plymouth Sound to begin a long, and draughty, flight back to Germany – and later fame as the originator and leader of the *'Wilde Sau'* nightfighter force (see *Osprey Aircraft of the Aces 20 - German Nightfighter Aces* for further details).

In an attempt to counter the hazards posed by barrage balloon defences, a number of Ju 88A-5s were fitted with cumbersome balloon-cable fenders and cutters. Designated the A-6, the resultant machine was not a success, for the extra weight and drag made it highly vulnerable to fighter interception. It was quickly withdrawn, with most aircraft of this type having the fender removed and reverting to normal bomber operations . . .

. . . as did this machine, which has become thoroughly bogged down in the soft surface of a grass airfield. The only evidence of its former role are the small fairings behind the nose glazing, which were the attachment points for the fender as seen in the preceding photograph

The first week of August remained relatively quiet for the Ju 88 *Gruppen*, although single machines failed to return from as far apart as Cumberland and Devon. But in the 48 hours leading up to *'Adlertag'* ('Eagle Day'), the planned knockout blow against Fighter Command's airfields, the Junkers were to suffer their first significant losses of the campaign.

On 11 August KG 54 launched its first large-scale operation since converting to the Ju 88. It was aimed at 'harbour installations, the tank farm, torpedo depot and ships in Portland harbour'. Some 38 aircraft took part in the attack, the first leaving Evreux at 1035 hours. En route, they were joined by 20 He 111s of KG 27. With an escort of more than 100 Bf 109s and Bf 110s, it was the heaviest raid yet sent against the United Kingdom.

Forewarned by radar, the RAF responded in strength, with fighters from eight squadrons being directed against the attackers. While a massive dogfight filled the sky over Weymouth Bay, the bombers made for their targets. The Junkers hit at least one of their assigned objectives, diving on the oil storage farm and leaving two tanks ablaze. Perhaps as a result of their relative inexperience, this was one occasion when Ju 88 losses exceeded those of the Heinkels. Only one of the latter was brought down, whereas five of the Junkers failed to return – among them all three of II./KG 54's *Stabskette* machines.

A 'Totenkopf' machine undergoing maintenance in a camouflaged blast pen constructed from hay bales

One of the three aircraft lost by the *Gruppenstab* of II./KG 54 during the 11 August raid, 'B3+DC' forced-landed on Portland Head and is seen here under armed guard

KG 51 could hardly blame inexperience for the even heavier losses they suffered 24 hours later in a two-pronged attack on Portsmouth harbour and the Isle of Wight. In a further escalation of the Luftwaffe's offensive, KG 51's raid was a maximum effort by 90 Ju 88s from all three *Gruppen*, escorted by nearly 150 fighters.

But Fighter Command had learned a lesson over Portland the previous day. This time they tried to ignore the fighter escort, keeping their sights firmly fixed on the bombers instead. KG 51 paid a heavy price, with 12 of

A close-up of a KG 51 machine showing the elaborate hand-painted 'Edelweiss' unit badge which was retained throughout the war, and which, in miniature form, was still adorning the *Geschwader's* Me 262 jets at its close

Although the date at the top is suspect (some sources have suggested that it has been altered from '13.8.40', and that this is, in fact, KG 54's operations board for *'Adlertag'* itself), it is interesting to note that, in addition to the main force of 36 Ju 88s, the 'Totenkopf' *Geschwader* also operated its own He 111s for air-sea rescue duties

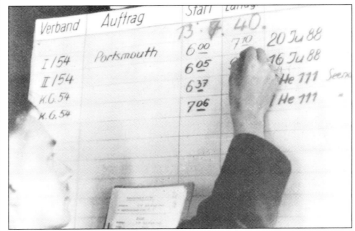

Five KG 54 aircraft forced- or belly-landed back in France after the *'Adlertag'* missions of 13 August. It is not known whether this particular machine was one of them. The bullet-holed fuselage clearly bears the marks of battle, but it is something down by the starboard propeller blade which has captured the interest of these pioneers from the RAD (Reich's Labour Service)

its aircraft being lost, including that of the *Geschwaderkommodore*, Oberst Dr Johann-Volkmar Fisser, who was leading the 20 machines which had broken off from the main force to attack the radar station at Ventnor, on the Isle of Wight.

By contrast, on *'Adlertag'* itself, 13 August, the Ju 88 *Gruppen* escaped fairly lightly. During early-morning raids against Odiham and Farnborough, I. and II./KG 54 lost just two aircraft apiece (although many more were damaged), whilst that afternoon a pair of Junkers from III./LG 1 were shot down while attacking Andover. Twenty-four hours later it was I./LG 1's turn to lose a brace of Ju 88s – both reportedly claimed by Spitfire ace Flt Lt Robert Stanford Tuck of No 92 Sqn in the space of five minutes – during an early evening hit-and-run aid on Middle Wallop.

The following evening LG 1 returned to the same sector station in greater strength – some 30 of their Junkers again attacking Middle Wallop, while an equal number targeted Worthy Down. No fewer than eight of the bombers fell victim to the defending fighters. But these were not the only Ju 88 losses to be suffered by the Luftwaffe on 15 August. This day had seen massed raids launched by all three of the *Luftflotten* engaged in the Battle, including *Luftflotte* 5 from its bases in Scandinavia.

The first – and last – serious attempt to strike at the 'rear' of Fighter Command's defences by mounting an early afternoon attack across the North Sea against airfields in north-east England was not a success. *Luftflotte* 5 sent its bombers over in two waves. To the north, aiming for the Newcastle-upon-Tyne area, went the He 111s of KG 26, escorted by a single *Zerstörergruppe* (see *Osprey Aircraft of the Aces 25 - Messerschmitt Bf 110 Zerstörer Aces of World War 2* for further details). Further south, about 50 Junkers of KG 30 – a mix of bombers and Ju 88C heavy fighters – targeted fighter stations at Church Fenton and Leconfield, in Yorkshire.

Once again the Luftwaffe's intelligence was at fault. They were firmly convinced that northern England had been all but denuded of its fighter squadrons to sustain the battle being waged over the southern counties. But they were wrong. Approaching Flamborough Head, and still some ten miles (16 km) out to sea, the Ju 88s were suddenly bounced by a dozen Spitfires from No 616 Sqn, backed up by a flight of No 73 Sqn Hurricanes (see *Osprey Aircraft of the Aces 18 - Hurricane Aces 1939-40* for further details).

One of the Junkers' crew members wrote an account which was later published in the Luftwaffe Yearbook;

'Visibility had become very poor. Sea and sky merged with no sign of an horizon. It was misty, but the English coastline should appear below us at any moment.

'Still nothing to be seen. Aircraft all round us, gently undulating. Our target; an English airfield. What would it look like? We were familiar with its layout from the reconnaissance photos – every hangar, every barrack block.

'"The coast!" – no more time for day-dreaming.

'"Fighters to starboard!" Three tiny dots flying high above us. They disappear astern, and then dive down on our tail.

'Our machine guns fire short bursts at the leading fighter. He breaks away and the second one takes his place. He too fails to hit us.

'"Five fighters to port above", reports the wireless operator calmly – we continue to head for our target, trying to spot it among the now broken cloud. "There, below us, the field!"

'The target at last – the aircraft noses over into a dive, speed building up rapidly, the wind howling and roaring. The hangars grow in size. The flak is intense.

'A jolt, and the bombs fall free. Down below all hell is let loose. Hangar walls and roofs crumple like tinfoil, wreckage flies through the air, aircraft are torn apart by shrapnel, huge clouds of smoke and dust rise like giant mushrooms, shot through by more flames and explosions.'

Couched in the style of the period, Oberleutnant Rudolf Kratz's words no doubt reflected his personal impressions of the raid. But they did not reveal the entire truth. Shortly before reaching Leconfield, the Junkers had suddenly veered south and attacked instead the Bomber Command airfield at Driffield. It was this station's 20 anti-aircraft guns which were responsible for the 'intense' barrage which greeted the raiders.

The damage inflicted on the ground was severe, and included the destruction of nine Whitley bombers (from Nos 77 and 102 Sqns). But Kratz's account, not surprisingly, fails to mention his own unit's losses. Seven of KG 30's Junkers – five of them Ju 88C fighters – were shot down, and three others crashed or forced-landed upon return.

The 15 aircraft lost by LG 1 and KG 30 on 15 August 1940 were to be the highest single day's casualties ever suffered by the Ju 88 *Kampfgruppen* over Great Britain.

The month of August ended as it had begun for the Junkers' crews – fairly uneventfully and with combat losses kept to a minimum, except on two occasions. On 21 August six Ju 88s were brought down, two of them being machines of KGr 806 (each commanded by a naval Leutnant), which were lost off Cornwall. All but one of 24 August's five casualties were II./KG 76 aircraft shot down while attacking Manston. Among those killed was *Gruppenkommandeur* Major Möricke.

The next multiple losses did not occur until 9 September, when five KG 30 machines failed to return. Listed among the missing was another *Gruppenkommandeur*, but III./KG 30's Major Hackbarth survived a ditching in the Channel to become a prisoner-of-war.

No doubt about this victim of Britain's northern defences. 7./KG 30's *'Dora-Richard'* was one of the seven 'Eagle' *Geschwader* aircraft brought down during the raid over Yorkshire on 15 August. Now it serves as a handy perch for a publicity shot of trainee fighter pilots

KG 30's objective on that 9 September had been London's docks, for by now the emphasis of the aerial onslaught against Great Britain had undergone a radical change. The Luftwaffe was no longer concentrating on neutralising the RAF's airfields, preparatory to invasion (the first time in the war that this prerequisite to a successful *Blitzkrieg* had been abandoned before it had achieved its object). German bombs inadvertently dropped on Greater London during the night of 24/25 August had prompted the RAF to retaliate in kind on Berlin. This in turn had so incensed the Führer that he ordered Göring to mount a round-the-clock bombing offensive against England's capital.

The *Kampfgeschwader* of *Luftflotte* 2, based in north-eastern France and the Low Countries, would attack London by day. Those of *Luftflotte* 3, further to the west, would do so under cover of darkness. It was to bolster *Lfl.* 2's strength that KG 30 had been transferred down from Denmark (shortly after the costly raid across the North Sea on 15 August) to airfields in the Netherlands. The anti-shipping veterans of the 'Eagle' *Geschwader* – long used to the open expanses of the North Sea – found a very different war awaiting them over southern England.

Generalfeldmarschall Albert Kesselring's *Luftflotte* 2 was reinforced by four more Ju 88 *Kampfgruppen* at this juncture, one of these being III./KG 1 – the first *Gruppe* of the 'Hindenburg' *Geschwader* to convert from the He 111. The other three were the component *Gruppen* of KG 77.

This latter *Geschwader* had already acquired something of a reputation as a 'hard-luck outfit', having suffered considerable losses in earlier campaigns. In fact, two of its Do 17s shared the dubious distinction of being the first Luftwaffe aircraft shot down in World War 2, and after one of its opening forays over south-east England in early July 1940, five Dorniers were reported missing. Since then KG 77 had contributed more than its fair share of Ju 88 training casualties as it re-equipped in the Homeland. And in just two raids over England in the latter half of September, KG 77's losses would account for almost 40 per cent of the entire month's Ju 88 combat casualty figures!

The first of these operations was a fast raid by III./KG 77 aimed at Tilbury Docks on the afternoon of 18 September. Approaching up the Thames Estuary, the still relatively inexperienced Ju 88 crews were set upon by close on 100 RAF fighters. They lost nine aircraft – five from 8. *Staffel* alone – in very short order. Two of those killed were *Gruppenkommandeur* Major Maxim Kless and a Luftwaffe war correspondent who

Back to the south and to KG 54 for the next unfortunate, 'B3+BM' of the 'Totenkopf's' 4. *Staffel*, bellied disconsolately in a Sussex farmer's field after suffering damage from both AA fire and Hurricane fighters on 21 August. Souvenir hunters have already stripped the tail of its swastikas. A later arrival on the scene, the senior fighter controller of nearby Tangmere is seen here organising something of more practical use – a tankful of illicit aviation fuel for that rather nice Bentley!

Less than three weeks later, and only five miles (eight kilometres) to the east, Major Hackbarth, *Gruppenkommandeur* of III./KG 30, would ditch his *'Anton-Dora'* in shallow water off Pagham harbour

had made the mistake of going along on the raid to record the unit's 'baptism of fire' with its new mounts.

Nine days later, on 27 September, the combined strengths of I. and II./KG 77 suffered an even worse mauling. The 55 Ju 88s missed the rendezvous with their fighter escort over the Channel, and again inexperience showed, for the two *Gruppen* continued on regardless in

KG 77's unit badge was based on the banner and motto of medieval German knighthood. Unfortunately, the *Geschwader's* performance did not always match up to that of its illustrious forbears

57

KG 77 crews relax in the sun at Laon-Athies as they await their next mission. 5. *Staffel's* '3Z+HN' in the background wears white formation bars on its rudder and port upper wing surfaces

faultless formation, but completely unprotected, across Kent towards their given objective – south London.

This time there were even more defending fighters (some 120 Hurricanes and Spitfires in all) waiting to pounce upon the close-ranked bombers. Only now did the Junkers break radio silence. Frantic appeals for assistance brought large numbers of Bf 109s on to the scene, but they were too late to stop the Ju 88s being scattered across the southern counties and losing 12 of their number as they sought to regain the comparative safety of the Channel.

The wreckage of the KG 77 machines strewn across Kent and Surrey effectively signalled the end of the Ju 88's part in the Battle of Britain. In fact, the entire daylight bombing offensive was rapidly winding down. By early October – finding no protection in numbers against the tenacious, and seemingly inexhaustible, RAF fighters – the Luftwaffe was beginning to despatch bombers singly, or in small groups, to make hit-and-run raids on specific targets.

Although this new tactic reduced October's losses to little more than a steady trickle, it did not stop them altogether. Among the first victims was a machine of the *Stab* I./KG 77 briefed to attack Woodley airfield, near Reading, on the morning of 3 October. Losing their way in the poor visibility, the crew found themselves north of London, where they chanced upon the de Havilland aircraft works at Hatfield.

From an altitude of only 50 ft (15 m), Oberleutnant Siegward Fiebig swept across the adjoining airfield, machine-gunning as he went and 'skip-bombing' his four 250-kg bombs off the wet grass and into the sheet metal shop and the work's technical school. The Ju 88 was met by a hail of anti-aircraft fire – everything from 40 mm Bofors shells to bullets from an antiquated Hotchkiss machine-gun wielded by the enthusiastic local Home Guard. It could not withstand this combined mistreatment, and crashed some six miles (ten kilometres) away.

All four crew members survived to become prisoners-of-war, not knowing that amongst the damage they had wrought was the destruction of much of the material being assembled for the production of the RAF's new Mosquito bomber, the first prototype of which would fly in just six weeks' time.

Twenty-four hours later I./KG 77 lost another aircraft. It went down in the sea off the Suffolk coast to provide the seventh victory of the Battle claimed by Stanford Tuck, who was now a squadron leader flying Hurricanes as the commanding officer of No 257 Sqn. But it was not just the 'tyros' who were sustaining casualties during this period, for the experienced KG 30 and LG 1 both suffered losses as October progressed. Indeed, the last Ju 88 combat casualty of the month was a machine of III./LG 1 downed over Cambridgeshire by Hurricanes from No 1 Sqn.

By now, in order to minimise further bomber losses by day particularly among the vulnerable Do 17 and He 111-equipped *Kampfgruppen*, the Luftwaffe was resorting more and more to high-altitude fighter-bomber sorties to continue the daylight offensive. The air war over Britain by night, hitherto primarily the responsibility of *Luftflotte* 3 (most of whose casualties over the past weeks had occurred in crashes while attempting to land back in France in the dark!) would soon be expanded to include almost the entire bomber strength based in occupied western Europe.

The Luftwaffe regarded this as a continuation of the campaign they had begun back in July. They had simply shifted the weight of their attack from daylight to darkness. For the defenders, however, it marked the end of the Battle and the start of a new offensive against their beleaguered isle. The events of the coming months added a new word to the English vocabulary – the 'Blitz'.

NIGHT BLITZ

From late 1940 onwards almost all Ju 88 activity over the United Kingdom was to be shrouded in

As summer turned to autumn there were fewer opportunities to sunbathe. Instead, aircraft such as this unidentified Ju 88 – ready armed with four 250-kg bombs – had to be protected against the elements

A survivor of the late summer battles, this A-5 of 2./KG 77 is also well wrapped up, with only its own reflection for company as it sits in the slush of a mist-shrouded Laon-Athies

darkness. The Junkers would be often heard, but seldom seen – except by the electronic 'eyes' of British radar, or as twisted piles of wreckage in the cold light of morning.

At first, however, during the winter months of 1940-41, the Luftwaffe bombers left little evidence of their nightly passage other than the damage

Caught by ground fire during a low-level attack on the Bomber Command airfield at Linton-on-Ouse, in north Yorkshire, in the early evening of 27 October 1940, 7./KG 4's *'Emil-Richard'* struggled nearly 100 miles (160 km) back towards the coast before finally being forced to belly-land. A soldier points the obligatory finger at the *Staffel's* recently-introduced badge, which reflects its new nocturnal deployment

This bellied-in Junkers has attracted quite a crowd of civilian sightseers. The badge on the bullet-riddled nose identifies it as a machine belonging to 2./KGr. 806

Forty-eight hours later another *'Gustav'* of the 'Edelweiss' *Geschwader*, '9K+GT' of 9./KG 51 (Wk-Nr 7062, which is the machine in the middle of this *Kette* of A-1s), was written off in a landing accident at III. *Gruppe's* Brétigny base

This badly damaged Ju 88A-1 of II./KG 51 ('9K+FP'?) managed to make it back across the Channel on one engine before belly-landing in northern France. Note the bullet holes in the fuselage and starboard wingroot, and the feathered propeller of the starboard engine . . .

. . . while a close-up of the nose reveals another bullet hole in the pilot's side window. It also shows his contoured, armoured seat – back-to-back with the smaller bucket seat provided for the wireless-operator/rear gunner – and graphically illustrates the narrow confines of the Ju 88's cockpit

– often severe – which they themselves had inflicted on London or on some unfortunate provincial town or city. Very few of their own number were brought down, for the RAF's nightfighter arm was still in its infancy, and the thousands of shells sent up by the AA guns did more good for civilian morale than harm to the enemy overhead.

For example, in arguably one of the most infamous raids of this period – the attack on Coventry on the night of 14/15 November, when Ju 88s made up almost half of the 300-strong attacking force – only one of the raiders was brought down, the hapless Do 17 of KG 3 being struck by AA fire. And although the one enduring image of this night's raid will always be the hollow, burnt-out shell of the city's St Michael's cathedral, other, more legitimate, targets were also hard hit. Coventry housed the Fleet Air Arm's main stores depot, and whether by chance or design, this was heavily bombed and completely destroyed. The effects, according to one informed source, 'were felt by Swordfish squadrons all over the world'.

Of the dozen Ju 88s which failed to return from night operations over

The tail section of 6./KG 77's '3Z+EP' – the mysterious crewless Ju 88A-5 which crashed near Redhill, in Surrey, in the early hours of 28 November 1940

Britain in November 1940, only four came down on English soil, and only two of them were claimed by the ground defences. Another, 3./KG 54's 'Victor-Ludwig', which crashed near Chichester in the early hours of 20 November, provided what is believed to be the first recorded victory for a radar-equipped Beaufighter.

But it was the last of the month's losses – an aircraft from II./KG 77 whose tail unit had broken off after it hit power cables south-east of

An unidentified *'Berta'* of KG 1 follows a sister-ship out on to the darkened runway at the start of another night raid. Note the full load of underwing bombs

The large hornet carried below the cockpit of this A-5 identifies it as a machine of the *Gruppenstab* III./KG 76, which began conversion onto the Junkers during the winter of 1940-41

Redhill early in the morning of 28 November – which baffled RAF intelligence officers. Although scribbled notes found among the wreckage indicated that the crew had experienced some sort of serious trouble (one read simply 'Pass round – bale out'), there were no reports of any parachutists landing in England that night.

It was some time before the facts became known. The crew had indeed abandoned their aircraft – but over Reims in France. Left to its own devices the bomber had thereupon circled back on its tracks and re-crossed the Channel, before finally coming to earth in Surrey!

December's only losses both occurred during another major raid on London on the night of 8/9, single machines from both KG 77 and LG 1 falling victim to anti-aircraft fire over Essex. It is uncertain whether the following month's sole nocturnal Ju 88 casualty – an aircraft of I./LG 1 which failed to return from a raid on Avonmouth on 16/17 January 1941 – was also attributable to ground defences, or to the heavy snow showers and associated poor visibility over the West Country that night.

By this time a number of organisational changes had taken place. All *Luftflotte* 2's Ju 88 units had been transferred to the control of

Luftflotte 3 for the continuation of the night bombing offensive against the United Kingdom, and with two more *Gruppen* (II./KG 1 and III./KG 76) now having completed conversion to the Junkers, this meant that 14 of the 27 *Kampfgruppen* subordinated to *Lftl.* 3 were equipped with the Ju 88. Late in January 1941 that total rose to 15 when I./KG 76 exchanged the last of its Do 17s for Junkers.

This would be the largest force of Ju 88s ever ranged against Great Britain, for already the first Junkers units were being withdrawn from occupied western Europe. The Führer's plans for a seaborne invasion of southern England, never wholehearted, had finally been shelved altogether. His attention was now turning to other areas of conquest.

Among the first to depart was the Luftwaffe's premier Ju 88 unit. Admittedly, the 'Eagle' *Geschwader* did not move far, simply transferring from the Netherlands into neighbouring north-west Germany (and thence back up into Scandinavia). KG 30 had already undergone some internal changes of its own, for at the end of 1940 III./KG 30 had been re-assigned as an operational training unit. The vacant III. *Gruppe* slot was in turn filled by redesignating the Ju 88-equipped III./KG 4 (who were to lose three aircraft during a daylight anti-shipping mission over the Thames Estuary on 16 January 1941).

While KG 30 resumed their activities over the drab greyness of the North Sea – attacking inshore shipping and coastal towns both by day and night – the Junkers of II. and III./LG 1 were despatched to sunnier climes. By the middle of that same January some 50 of their number were based at Catania in Sicily – the vanguard of the Ju 88's long association with the Mediterranean theatre. Within weeks they would be joined on Sicily by III./KG 30, while I./LG 1 and KG 51 were ordered to south-east Europe late in March in preparation for the campaign in the Balkans.

Despite this reduction in its strength, and before the mass exodus of bomber units eastwards in the early summer of 1941 (part of the build-up of forces for the forthcoming invasion of the Soviet Union) robbed

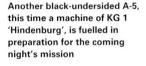

Another black-undersided A-5, this time a machine of KG 1 'Hindenburg', is fuelled in preparation for the coming night's mission

KG 1's use of black distemper was not restricted to the undersurfaces of their aircraft. They also used it to entirely obliterate all national insignia and unit markings. Only the re-application of this machine's 'last two' in tiny white characters on the rear fuselage reveal that Wk-Nr 3332 is, in fact, 9. *Staffel's 'Heinrich-Theodor'*

A bomb-laden A-5 of KG 1 climbs away into the evening sky, watched by an armed sentry and a solitary 'black man' still working on another of the *Geschwader's* machines

Although KG 1 were meticulous in camouflaging their aircraft for night operations, they retained their unit badge – a facsimile of the signature of the late President Hindenburg, a World War 1 hero in whose honour the *Geschwader* had been named on 20 April 1936

Luftflotte 3 of its *Kampfgruppen* almost entirely, the Luftwaffe in the west mounted one last series of raids against the British Isles.

Initially, these were carried out by small formations of bombers sent to attack widely separated targets. The first of three aircraft to be lost in February 1941 was an aircraft from 8./KG 1 which landed almost intact in Cambridgeshire following a night raid on Liverpool in the early hours of 16 February. Forty-eight hours later another machine from the very same *Staffel*, together with one of 6./KG 76's Ju 88s, failed to return from a daylight mission flown against targets along the East Coast.

Still relative newcomers to the Ju 88, KG 76 also suffered two of the seven casualties reported in the first half of March. Both these machines were lost on the same night of 12/13, one over Liverpool and the other while attacking Portsmouth. The following night witnessed the first combat loss for *Küstenfliegergruppe* 106, – another of the ex-naval flying-boat units now converted on to the Ju 88 (but still operating under its original coastal designation). This too met its end over the East Coast.

Twenty-four hours later still, Liverpool was again the target for a Junkers of KGr 806, which was shot down by a Beaufighter.

Although weather conditions were still far from perfect, mid-March was to witness an upsurge in activity as Luftwaffe raids grew in strength and intensity. On the night of 15/16 March 100+ bombers were despatched against London. The following night close on 200 Heinkels and Junkers made a two-pronged attack on Bristol and the neighbouring

Many hands make light work. A crowd of 'black men' have anchored a block and tackle to the tailwheel of this Ju 88A-4 and are using muscle power to hoist a 1800-kg (4000-lb) 'Satan' bomb up onto the underwing rack. Coded 'M2+AK', the machine is almost certainly the mount of the *Staffelkapitän* of 2./KüFlGr 106

The all-NCO crew of 9./KG 76's *'Bertha-Theodor'*, photographed before taking off for a raid on Liverpool on the evening of 12 March 1941. When their starboard engine nacelle was set alight by AA fire over the target area, all four baled out to become PoWs for the duration

An A-5 of 9./KG 1, which is again identifiable only by the tiny 'last two' on the rear fuselage. Aircraft 'GT' compromises its otherwise toned-down finish (including black paint splashed over wing and tail upper surfaces and along the fuselage spine) by displaying at least half-a-dozen white mission symbols on its tailfin

Avonmouth docks. The sole casualty to come down over the United Kingdom was a KG 51 machine which suffered a double engine failure.

There followed major raids on Hull, Southampton, Plymouth and London before the weather closed in again at month's end and brought a virtual halt to all nocturnal activity. April 1941 began quietly but soon escalated into a nightly succession of devastating attacks. Once again provincial towns and cities, particularly the ports and harbours, suffered heavily. Clydeside, Tyneside, Liverpool, Bristol and Belfast were all targeted, as too were Birmingham and Coventry.

But again and again the raiders returned to London. On the night of 16/17 April *Luftflotte* 3 mounted a major attack on the capital. Over 500 bombers (nearly 300 of them Ju 88s) were despatched in three waves. Severe damage was caused in this, the heaviest raid of the war to date. It cost the Luftwaffe five Ju 88s – a quarter of the month's total Junkers casualties – plus a solitary He 111. Three of the Ju 88s, all from KG 77, may have succumbed to flak. The other two, from KG 1 and KG 76, were both claimed by No 219 Sqn Beaufighters, as was the Heinkel.

By now the night Blitz was rapidly approaching its climax. The past weeks and months had been a testing time for those living in the larger urban areas of Great Britain. Thousands had been killed. But the Luftwaffe's nocturnal offensive had done little to further Germany's cause militarily.

With the evening sun casting a long shadow on the engine nacelle above their heads, KG 1 groundcrew prepare another of their charges. Note the 'screamers' on the tailfins of the bomb between the two men in the foreground, and the stripe (painted in yellow) which identifies it as a thin-cased GP type

Another machine which failed to return from a raid on Liverpool. I./KG 30's '4D+BH' was attacked by a Defiant nightfighter in the early hours of 3 May. It made it back as far as the east coast before belly-landing on a Norfolk beach

For the crews of the Ju 88s it had been a period of sustained effort, interrupted only by the spells of bad weather. Each *Gruppe* had to locate and attack a wide range of targets the length and breadth of a blacked-out Britain. Sometimes they flew more than one mission on the same night. And while the cost had not been prohibitive, their losses had been slowly increasing all the while. They came to a head in May 1941. That month's 40+ aircraft lost was the highest total since the daylight Battle of the previous summer.

Seven of those casualties were suffered on the night of 4/5 May alone, aircraft being brought down during, or after, raids as far apart as Belfast, Bridlington and Torquay. But its was the devastating attack on London, lasting a full seven hours during the night of 10/11 May 1941, which brought to a close the Luftwaffe's almost year-long attempt to subjugate the British from the air.

Although none of the 250+ participating Ju 88s were lost that night, another 23 would fail to return from lesser raids before the month was out. By then, however, the mass move eastwards had begun. The Luftwaffe was about to attempt over the Russian steppe what it had signally failed to do over the Kentish Downs – blow the enemy's air force out of the sky.

By anybody's yardstick the Battle of Britain was well and truly over.

MARITIME WAR

Little more than a week after London's seven-hour ordeal by fire, a very different drama began to unfold. In the early hours of 19 May the German battleship *Bismarck* sailed from Gotenhafen in the Baltic. The pride of the Kriegsmarine was on her maiden voyage, out into the vastness of the Atlantic Ocean to prey on Britain's lifeline convoys.

Although spotted by a Coastal Command reconnaissance aircraft as she steamed northwards along the Norwegian coast, the 41,700-ton giant

Aircraft of the *Gruppenstab* I./KG 30 ('4D+CB' in the foreground and 'EB' behind) at their base in Norway. The number of bombs of all types left lying in the open ready for use indicate that – unlike in northern France – here there was little fear of surprise enemy air attack

was safely shepherded on her way by units of the Luftwaffe, including the Ju 88s of I. and II./KG 30. Soon she was well beyond their range, entering the Denmark Strait north-west of Iceland, but shadowed now by two Royal Navy cruisers.

Fearing the havoc she could cause once astride the major convoy routes, the Admiralty despatched the main body of the Home Fleet from Scapa Flow to intercept her. In an historic series of actions the *Bismarck* first sank HMS *Hood*, the world's largest battlecruiser, before she herself was subjected to a succession of surface and air attacks from other units of the Britsih Fleet.

Crippled by shell and torpedo hits, the *Bismarck* set course south-eastwards for the French Atlantic coast and the safety of an air umbrella. Unfortunately, nobody had had the foresight to transfer the two anti-shipping *Gruppen* of KG 30 down from Norway to Western France to cover her arrival and, hopefully, see off her pursuers.

The local Air Command, the *Fliegerführer Atlantik,* was primarily a reconnaissance force. Its only striking power was provided by a dozen long-range, but vulnerable, Fw 200 Condors and some 16 serviceable Ju 88s of yet another of those ex-coastal units now operating as autonomous *Kampfgruppe* – KGr 606. This unit, incidentally, had suffered its first two operational Ju 88 casualties over the West Country early on the morning of 19 May – the same time, almost to the minute, that the *Bismarck* was slipping her moorings in Gotenhafen.

Although experienced coastal flyers, the aircrews of KGr 606 had been trained to shadow and attack merchant shipping, not face the full might of the enemy's main battle fleet. Nevertheless, eight Junkers took off on the morning of 27 May to seek the stricken *Bismarck* and render what

A formation of 'Eagle' *Geschwader* A-5s over the inhospitable Norwegian landscape

assistance they could. Five of them picked up her direction-finding signals and an hour later found the battleship fighting her last against overwhelming odds.

The Ju 88s tried unsuccessfully to dive-bomb a Royal Navy cruiser, but as the crews later reported, they were hindered in their attempts 'by strong interference from "Gladiator aircraft". The Junkers had presumably stumbled across Swordfish torpedo-bombers from the *Ark Royal*, out hunting the *Bismarck*, which they mistook for biplane fighters!

By the time Luftwaffe reinforcements (in the shape of II./KG 1, II./KG 54 and I./KG 77) arrived in western France it was too late. The *Bismarck* was at the bottom of the Atlantic. The three Ju 88 *Gruppen* were sent out after the retiring British ships but failed to find them.

The Junkers' role in the sorry saga of the *Bismarck* could hardly be described as pivotal. But, far to the north, the anti-shipping Ju 88s of KG 30 would play an important part in the protracted campaign against the Arctic convoys transporting war material to the Soviet Union. Although fought mainly against the western allies, much of the action would take place to the east of Bear Island as the convoys neared their Russian ports of destination, and are thus more properly part of the story of the Junkers Ju 88 in the east.

But before becoming fully committed to the war in the Arctic, I. and II./KG 30 continued to operate around the British coastline. For the latter half of 1941 and into the early months of 1942 – from bases in Scandinavia and while on temporary detachment to the Low Countries – KG 30 was the sole Ju 88 *Kampfgeschwader* to remain in action against the British Isles. Its two *Gruppen* were, however, supported by three of the ex-coastal units in the form of *Kampfgruppen* 106, 506 and 606. A fourth,

A flurry of activity at 1./KGr 506's dispersal presages an imminent operation. In the foreground, already bombed-up, is 'S4+OH', Wk-Nr 2084

KGr 906, was engaged predominantly on air-sea rescue duties.

Nine months of anti-shipping operations – both mining and attacking vessels in Britain's coastal waterways – exacted a steady toll of all these units. Some 60+ Junkers failed to return from missions during this period, a large proportion of this total being claimed by the RAF's much improved nightfighter arm. Others succumbed to the pugnacious anti-aircraft gunners aboard HM trawlers.

The pilot of this night-camouflaged A-1 from KGr 806 got safely back to base despite severe anti-aircraft damage to his port elevator

Ju 88A-5 'M2+MK' (Wk-Nr 6073) of 2./KGr 106 landed in error at Chivenor, in Devon, on the evening of 26 November 1941. It is seen here at the USAAF fighter base of Goxhill, in Lincolnshire, in 1943-44, having become HM509 of the RAF's No 1426 (Enemy Aircraft) Flight. The Ju 88 survived until 19 May 1944, when it was ground-looped at RAF Thorney Island, on the Hampshire coast. Although not seriously damaged in the aborted take-off accident, the bomber was nonethelss brocken up for spare parts, with its engines going to another captured Ju 88 operated by the Flight

But German aircrews faced a more insidious enemy in the night skies over and around Great Britain – the 'Meacon' radio countermeasures system, which mimicked and falsified the signals emanating from the Luftwaffe's own navigational radio beacons. An unknown number of Ju 88s were deceived by this piece of electronic chicanery. On the night of 9/10 July 1941, for example, three machines of KGr 106, believing

themselves to be over the North Sea, flew into the ground in Yorkshire. Exactly a fortnight later two I./KG 30 aircraft were also well and truly 'Meaconed', one landing at an RAF airfield near Weston-super-Mare with the crew convinced they were safely back in France. Another Ju 88 was delivered intact into the RAF's hands on the evening of 26 November when a KGr 106 machine put down at Chivenor, in Devon, after falling prey to a 'Meacon' beam over the Irish Sea.

Then, in the spring of 1942, the air war over Great Britain suddenly took on a new twist, with a whole new cast of Ju 88 units attacking a wholly new kind of target.

THE BAEDEKER RAIDS

On the night of 28/29 March 1942 RAF Bomber Command struck the Baltic seaport of Lübeck. Tacitly conceding that its aircraft were still incapable of finding pin-point targets in the dark, the aiming point for the night's raid was the city's *Altstadt*, or 'old town', an area of narrow, cobbled streets and half-timbered medieval houses.

Together with high explosives, more than 250 tons of incendiaries were dropped. It was estimated that over a quarter of the ancient city's built-up area was destroyed, including many buildings of cultural and historical importance. Since described as the 'first major success for Bomber Command', the Germans regarded it as a *Terrorangriff* (terror attack), pure and simple.

Ignoring certain obvious precedents – such as Warsaw, Rotterdam and Coventry – an enraged Hitler again demanded reprisals in kind. Britain's own historic cities were to be attacked without mercy. The Luftwaffe's attempts to comply with the Führer's wishes would become known as the *Baedeker* raids, after the famous nineteenth-century German tourist guidebooks of the same name which listed and described Britain's centres of cultural interest.

Caught in the photographer's flash-light, a Junkers crew are helped into their parachutes . . .

But putting *Baedeker* into practice was not going to be easy. Since the heady days of 1940, when *Luftflotte* 3 contributed over half the attackers engaged in the battle of Britain, that Command had been pared to the bone and transformed into an almost entirely defensive force. It was now concerned more with defending occupied northwest Europe against Allied incursions than taking the fight to the enemy's shores. Its sole offensive muscle comprised a handful of Dornier Do 217s of III./KG 2 and two *Staffeln* of fighter-bombers.

With the Luftwaffe fully stretched on the eastern and southern fronts, desperate measures were called for – and taken. Unlike the RAF's system of separate Operational Training Units (OTU), which was the final stage of schooling undergone by most British and Commonwealth trainee aircrew before their posting to any suitable first-line squadron, each Luftwaffe bomber unit operated its own internal equivalent of an OTU – usually organised as the *Geschwader's* fourth *Gruppe* – to provide its own replacement crews.

. . . as the mechanics prepare to start the starboard engine of their machine

Several of these IV. *Gruppen* were assigned to *Luftflotte* 3 to add their numbers to the *Baedeker* strike force. But the inexperience of the crews meant that many of their attacks were not pressed fully home. The main purpose of their presence in Britain's night skies was to draw attention away from the activities of KG 2's Dorniers. If any aerial opposition was encountered, their orders were to abort their mission and return to base.

Not all made it. On the night of 25/26 April 1942, during the second *Baedeker* raid on Bath, a Ju 88 of IV./KG 3 was caught by a No 255 Sqn Beaufighter and crashed into a Welsh hillside. Four nights later a IV./KG 77 machine failed to return from an attack on York, and on 3/4 May three trainee crews (two from IV./KG 30 and another from IV./KG 77) were lost during a heavy raid on Exeter.

Although a great trial for the citizens of England's cathedral cities and the other towns targeted, the *Baedeker* raids were achieving relatively little. Further attempts were made to bolster *Luftflotte* 3's strength. In May II. and III./KG 77 were transferred briefly to France. But the parlous situation in the south saw them returning to the Mediterranean just weeks later (not, however, before II./KG 77 – running true to form – had lost four aircraft in a single night during the 2/3 June raid on Canterbury).

The departing II. and III./KG 77 were replaced by I./KG 77 and II./KG 54, both from the eastern front. Arriving in July, the latter was

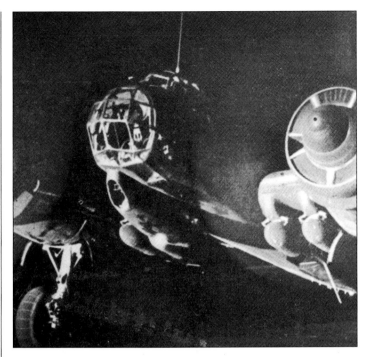

Engines running and all preflight checks complete, the fully-armed aircraft taxies out for take-off

hastily recalled to Russia in August.

By that time the *Baedeker* offensive was running out of steam. In the second of three consecutive night raids on the Midlands at the end of July two Ju 88s of III./KG 26 were brought down by AA fire. But these machines were not part of yet another *Gruppe* sent in to reinforce *Lfl.* 3's meagre strength. The original coastal unit, KüFlGr 506, had simply been subject to a second redesignation. After some 16 months operating as KGr 506, it had now become III./KG 26 (replacing the previous III./KG 26, which itself had been renumbered III./KG 28).

September 1942 saw offensive activity fall to an all-time low. Just two Ju 88s – both of I./KG 77 – were lost during an attack on Manchester on the night of 2/3. But in an attempt to inject new life into the failing air campaign against Great Britain, this month also witnessed the activation of a 'brand new *Kampfgeschwader* tasked solely with mounting operations over England'.

In fact, the *Geschwader* was not new at all. KG 6's three component *Gruppen* were 'created' by redesignating a trio of existing units – I./KG 77, KGr 106 and III./LG 1 respectively.

Nor was it used 'solely' against England. After a daylight raid on the east coast on 19 October, which cost II./KG 6 two aircraft, *Stab*, I. and II./KG 6 were rushed to the Mediterranean to counter Allied landings in north-west Africa.

Early in January 1943 *Stab* and I./KG 6 returned to northern France, where they were soon joined by III./KG 6 which had been serving on the eastern front. On the night of 17/18 January, during the first raid of any magnitude on London for many months, these two *Gruppen* lost four Ju 88s between them, all possibly falling victim to Beaufighters from No 29 Sqn. Apart from an extraordinary mission over northern Britain in the early hours of 25 March, when four KG 6 machines flew into high ground (and a fifth presumably came down in the sea), this was the highest single night's loss of the whole year.

Throughout most of 1943 KG 6 was the only Ju 88 bomber unit operating over the United Kingdom. During those 12 months, although they concentrated mainly on coastal targets, more than 60 of the *Geschwader's* aircraft would fail to return to their French and Belgian bases. But as the year progressed plans were being laid for one last major bombing offensive to be launched against the British Isles before the advent of the Führer's long promised, and much heralded, *Wunderwaffen* – unmanned V1 flying-bombs and supersonic V2 rockets – rendered such costly raids a thing of the past.

1944-45 - DECLINE AND DISSOLUTION

Angered by what he considered to be the 'mismanagement' of the air war against England to date, Hitler had ordered that one man should be appointed to oversee and conduct the coming offensive. From a number of candidates Göring selected Oberstleutnant Dietrich Peltz, who had been a Ju 87 Stuka pilot at the beginning of the war, but had since risen high in the ranks of the bomber arm.

Promoted to Oberst, Peltz had assumed the mantle of *Angriffsführer England* (Attack Leader England) towards the end of March

At just 29 years of age, Oberst Dietrich Peltz was the youngest Commanding General in the entire Wehrmacht. He is seen here wearing the Swords to the Oak Leaves of his Knight's Cross awarded on 23 July 1943

A night-camouflaged Ju 88S-1 of KG 6, pictured in the late summer of 1943

Aircrew don their life-jackets beneath the nose of a Ju 188A from 4./KG 66. Note the *'Kutonase'* balloon cable cutting device around the forward fuselage and the *Geschwader's* typical 'twin ring' spinner decoration

1943. Fully aware of the fact that with the slender forces at his immediate disposal – one understrength *Geschwader* of Ju 88s, another of Do 217s, and a third of Fw 190 fighter-bombers – he would be unable to trade the RAF's Bomber Command blow for blow, Peltz nevertheless set about his new task with a will.

One of the first measures he introduced was the activation of a special pathfinder unit, I./KG 66, initially equipped with a mix of Do 217s and Ju 88s. The latter included examples of the improved 'S' variant, re-engined and faster than the Ju 88A, but carrying less armour. Formed in April 1943, I./KG 66 lost its first Ju 88S late the following month when one of the new Junkers was shot down over Sussex by an No 85 Sqn Mosquito on the night of 29/30 May.

KG 6 also began to receive – and lose – examples of the aerodynamically refined Ju 88S as the summer turned to autumn. And by October 1943 both units were operating the even more radically new Ju 188, with its re-designed and extensively-glazed nose, sharply tapered wingtips and angular vertical tail surfaces.

Among the early Ju 188 casualties was a 2./KG 66 machine which crashed into the sea of the Yorkshire coast late in the evening of 2 October. In the middle of the month I./KG 6, which had converted fully onto the new type, lost three aircraft in one night, 15/16 October, all three being brought down over south-east England by Mosquitos of No 85 Sqn.

The greatly increased efficiency of Britain's nocturnal defences did not bode well for the forthcoming offensive, which was already suffering delays on account of the worsening weather. But Göring was determined to force the pace. In an order dated 3 December 1943 he stated his intention to intensify the air war against England in order to 'avenge the terror attacks by the enemy'.

To this end four more Ju 88 *Gruppen* were added to Peltz's strength – I. and II./KG 54, and I. and II./KG 30. In addition, KG 2, which had flown Dorniers throughout the war, had also begun a belated transition to Junkers aircraft. By the beginning of 1944 II./KG 2 was completely re-equipped with the Ju 188.

Code-named Operation *Steinbock* (Ibex), the offensive was finally launched on the evening of 21 January 1944 when the first of two waves of bombers was despatched against London. To the recipients of the Luftwaffe's attentions, the following weeks became known less cryptically –

This frontal close-up of 'Z6+KM' shows the *'Kutonase'* more clearly. Other points of interest are the exhaust flame dampers, the 20 mm MG 151 nose cannon and the more spacious (albeit also more exposed) cabin accommodation of the Ju 188

No wonder the 'black men' were among the fittest on the base! More brute strength being applied to hoist an SC 1000 heavy calibre bomb up on to *'Kurfürst-Martha's'* port underwing bomb shackles

A formation of Ju 188s of II./KG 2 head towards England early in 1944

With black undersides and disruptive blue-grey upper surface camouflage, a Ju 188 of an unidentified 1. *Staffel* (last two 'CH') braves the elements in the winter of 1943-44

Bottom
By comparison, this Ju 188E of I./KG 66 looks almost snug in one of the well-built, camouflaged hangars at its Montdidier base, south of Amiens

A closer look at an AB 1000 incendiary container, which could scatter more than 600 one-kilogram incendiary bomblets over a wide area. This photograph was taken at Varrelbusch in the spring of 1944. The meander-patterned Ju 88 in the background is believed to be an aircraft from KG 76

and certainly more accurately – as the 'Little', or 'Baby', Blitz. Given the limited number of Luftwaffe bombers involved, and the high state of readiness of Britain's defences (which by this stage extended beyond her coastline and included night-intruders patrolling the bomber's own bases waiting to attack them as they took off and landed), *Steinbock* stood little chance of achieving anything more than a local impact.

Sources differ as to the strengths of this first night's raids. The Luftwaffe claimed some 450 individual sorties were flown in the two waves. The British estimated that just 13 bombers reached Greater London – and this on a night which saw nearly 850 Bomber Command aircraft despatched against continental Europe!

Peltz may not have known the full details of his bombers' success – or lack of it – but he could not fail to be aware of their casualties. No fewer than 21 aircraft were lost, including 12 Junkers. A second *Steinbock* raid on the night of 29/30 January cost another 11, including a Ju 188 of I./KG 6 and a Ju 88S pathfinder of I./KG 66.

Another weapon widely used during 'Steinbock' was the high-explosive SC 1000, nicknamed the 'Hermann'. The ring welded around the nose of this bomb was designed to prevent it penetrating too deeply into the ground, thus maximising the blast effect

The morning of 19 April 1944, and an RAF crane clears the wreckage of 3./KG 54's *'Paula-Ludwig'*, which had forced-landed on the Fighter Command airfield at Bradwell Bay, in Essex, in the early hours, the crew believing they were safely back in Holland

Another casualty of that same night's raid – the last major attack to be flown against London during the war – was 'U5+KN' (code just visible below the tailfin swastika) of 5./KG 2. Shot down by a Mosquito nightfighter of No 85 Sqn, the Ju 188E crashed on farmland on Romney Marsh, in Kent

Despite this poor start, a further seven attacks were mounted during February, with that on the night of 18/19 being the heaviest suffered by Londoners since May 1941. But increased effort inevitably meant increased casualties. February's total of 48 Junkers lost was more than double that of the previous month.

The catalogue of losses lengthened during March, which would prove to be the costliest month of the *Steinbock* offensive with more than 50 Junkers destroyed over the course of six separate nights. On two of these Peltz diverted his *Kampfgruppen* away from the capital, purportedly targeting Hull on the 19/20 and Bristol on 27/28. But no bombs actually fell on either city.

On the night of 18/19 April 1944 London was subjected to its last major bombing raid of the war. Nearly half the attacking force of 125 aircraft reached and bombed the capital, and all but two of the 13 bombers lost were Junkers. It was the last time they would suffer double-figure casualties over England, for just like the ill-starred *Baedeker* raids of two years earlier, *Steinbock* too was now rapidly losing momentum.

For the remainder of April Peltz's *Gruppen* were restricted mainly to coastal targets, including Bristol and Portsmouth. The latter, crowded with invasion shipping gathering for D-Day, had to withstand a series of raids which continued into May. It was one such which cost *Steinbock* its highest-ranking casualty when, on the night of 22/23 May, the Ju 188 flown by Major Wilhelm Rath, *Geschwaderkommodore* of KG 2, was shot into the Channel south of the Isle of Wight by a nightfighter, believed to be a Mosquito of No 125 Sqn.

Exactly a fortnight later the landing craft which Rath and his crews had been attacking were pouring troops ashore on to the beaches of Normandy. The war had returned to mainland Europe.

Two shots of a Ju 188E from KG 66 in an unusual two-tone finish – black undersides with (apparently) overall blue-grey upper surfaces. Note the *'Kutonase'* rail and the absence of a dorsal turret. The only indication of the machine's actual identity are the minuscule 'last two' (letters 'TN') above the swastika on the tailfin. Although II./KG 66 was never officially activated, a 5. *Staffel* did exist for a few months during the summer/early autumn of 1944

With one wing pointing forlornly towards the sky, Ju 188A '3E+PH' from 1./KG 66 was found abandoned by the Allies at Melsbroek following the retreat of German forces from Belgium

NORMANDY

The eight depleted Junkers *Kampfgruppen* which had been participating in the closing stages of *Steinbock* no longer had to run the gauntlet of nightfighter patrols over the Channel in order to reach the hostile night skies over England. But the nocturnal airspace above the Normandy beach-heads would prove to be an even more dangerous environment. The two months following D-Day saw the virtual demise of the Junkers bomber force in the west.

KG 54 provides a prime example. The *Geschwader's* two surviving *Gruppen* (II./KG 54 having been disbanded in April) had ended May with just 12 serviceable Ju 88s between them. They were nevertheless ordered to mount a maximum effort on the first evening of the invasion, 6 June 1944. The Junkers attacked the easternmost of the landing beaches – the British 'Sword' – with 500-kg (1100-lb) fragmentation bombs.

'The target zone was dark and quiet. But the quietness was deceptive. As soon as the first bombs exploded a veritable inferno of flak erupted and searchlights stabbed into life, illuminating the barrage balloons above the ships.'

Five Ju 88s failed to return. These, and future, losses were quickly made good, but served only to prolong the agony. By the end of August KG 54 had lost a staggering 80 aircraft – four time its original strength of early June. The survivors were pulled out of the line and the *Geschwader* began converting to the Me 262 jet in September.

Within three weeks of the Normandy landings II./KG 2 did not have a single Ju 188 left. Although the *Gruppe* began receiving replacements in July, it – and the similarly equipped I./KG 2 – would be disbanded at the beginning of October.

KG 6, which had begun *Steinbock* with a full establishment of 110 Junkers, had been reduced to just 36 machines at its close. After three

weeks over Normandy this figure had been halved, and in September KG 6, too, was withdrawn from operations for conversion to Me 262 jet fighters.

Those two veteran anti-shipping units from the early months of the war over the North Sea, KGs 30 and 26, were also thrown into the maelstrom of the Normandy fighting.

Rarely mustering more than ten serviceable Ju 88s between them, II. and III./KG 30 were briefly transferred forward into Belgium from their north German bases in July. After several costly night attacks on Allied vessels off the invasion beaches and troop concentrations inland, the two *Gruppen* were withdrawn to central Europe, where the most experienced of their surviving pilots began retraining on single-engined fighters.

Staging northwards from their bases in southern France, the Ju 88 torpedo-bombers of II. and III./KG 26 also attempted to attack the mass of Allied shipping in the Channel by night. Although they claimed several ships sunk or damaged, the convoys' strong anti-aircraft defences – and the omnipresent nightfighters – prevented their achieving any significant results before the invasion of southern France in mid-August saw their hurried recall to the Mediterranean theatre.

An early *Mistel 1* combination as delivered to 2./KG 101. The upper component is a standard Bf 109F-4, whilst the lower consists of a Ju 88A-4 with a temporary nose section which would be replaced by a hollow-charge warhead prior to an operational mission

Operational *Mistel 1s*, believed to be from III./KG 66, pictured late in 1944. Note the 3500-kg (7800-lb) hollow-charge warheads which have been fitted in place of the standard Ju 88 crew cabins of the lower (bomber) components. It was *Misteln* such as these which took off to attack Scapa Flow

Just before midnight on 10 August a single Ju 88 *had* crossed the Channel, only to crash north of Andover, in Hampshire. The aircraft disintegrated completely upon impact, for it had been the lower component of a *Mistel* combination.

This somewhat bizarre weapon, which mated a single-engined fighter atop an unmanned bomber packed with explosives, had been under development for more than two years. It was intended as a means of attacking distant targets, the fighter being able to make additional use of the bomber's engines and fuel on the outward flight before releasing the missile and returning to base alone.

The one major objective in the west considered suitable for a *Mistel* raid was Scapa Flow, the Royal Navy's main fleet anchorage which had remained untroubled by anything other than the occasional reconnaissance snooper for over four years. The first operational *Mistel* unit, 2./KG 101, was formed in the spring of 1944. Based in Denmark, it was preparing for the attack on Scapa when the D-Day landings took place. Transferring to France, five *Misteln* carried out the weapon's first operational mission, against invasion shipping in the Seine Bay, on the night of 24/25 June. Four hits were claimed. It was during a similar sortie on 10/11 August, also aimed at Allied vessels in the Channel, that the Ju 88 mentioned above went astray, continuing to head northwards until coming to earth in Hampshire.

On the first night in September two more 'rogue' Ju 88s crashed, presumably by accident, on English soil – one fell in Kent and the other dived into the ground north of Mansfield, in Nottinghamshire, some 175 miles (280 km) from the Channel coast!

A crewman armed with a broom sweeps snow from the wing of a Ju 88S which has received a temporary meander-pattern winter camouflage over all surfaces, upper and lower. It is believed that these are aircraft from LG 1 pictured at the time of the Ardennes counter-offensive

By this time the *Mistel* force had been redesignated as III./KG 66. In October five *Misteln* of this unit were finally ready to launch the raid on Scapa Flow. Three came to grief before leaving Germany, and the remaining two failed to locate the target.

ARDENNES

Just three Junkers *Kampfgruppen* survived the bloodletting of the Normandy campaign to remain operational against the Western Allies until the very end of 1944.

I./KG 66, the *Steinbock* pathfinder unit, continued in this role throughout the Normandy fighting, despite seldom having more than

Two S-3s ('White H' nearest) of the same unit as seen on the previous page sit on the same snow-covered airfield, which has obviously seen a lot of activity since the previous photograph was taken during the winter 1944-45

Ju 88S-1 'Z6+NH' (note individual aircraft letter on wing inboard leading-edge) from 1./KG 66 undergoes a complete engine change – although the character in the foreground seems more concerned with repairing his bike!

Indicative of the chronic shortage of fuel, a team of oxen are used to haul the engineless 'Nordpol-Heinrich' through the winter mud

four or five of its Ju 188s serviceable at any one time. The Belgian-based I. and II./LG 1 were slightly better off. The *Geschwader's* III. *Gruppe* had been disbanded shortly before D-Day to help make up their numbers, and three weeks after the invasion they were still able to field 22 Ju 88s, divided evenly between them.

All three *Gruppen* received reinforcements during the months following the retreat from France, and each had over 20 aircraft on strength when they were called upon to provide support for Hitler's last great gamble in the west – the counter-offensive in the Ardennes.

Launched on 16 December 1944 along a 45-mile (72-km) stretch of lightly-held American front, the object of the surprise German counter-thrust was to cross the River Meuse and capture the supply port of Antwerp. This would cut the Anglo-American ground forces in two – a re-run, in fact, of the *Blitzkrieg* campaign of 1940, which had split the British BEF from the main body of the French.

This time, however, the Luftwaffe did not dominate the skies. The three Junkers *Gruppen* would operate under cover of darkness – singly or in small groups – flying mainly low-level nuisance raids against American ground columns on either flank of the growing 'Bulge'. One night, for example, they might be dropping fragmentation and anti-personnel bombs on US troop positions between Aachen and Verviers in the north, the next they would be harassing road convoys between Luxemburg and Metz to the south.

As well as helping to secure the flanks of the advance, there was one particular target to which the Junkers returned time and again – Bastogne. Held by the US 101st Airborne Division, this town had stood firm as the Panzers swept past it. Completely surrounded, Bastogne was subjected to nightly air raids. The first attack was delivered by 20+ Ju 88s of LG 1 on 23/24 December. The following night they were joined by I./KG 66's Ju 188s, who marked the town centre with flares. Nearly two tons of bombs were dropped, causing severe damage.

On 26/27 December LG 1 switched its attention to the line of the Meuse, bombing and strafing Allied targets in the path of the German advance. At least three of the nine aircraft engaged were brought down by AA fire, including the Ju 88S flown by the *Kommandeur* of I./LG 1, Hauptmann Rudiger Panneborg. However, their efforts were in vain, for the Panzers never did achieve their initial objective. They were halted just short of the Meuse on 27 December.

One of three *Misteln* caught by US P-51 Mustangs south of Hamburg on 3 February 1945, this Ju 88 lower component is recorded on the gun-camera film of the attacking fighter as it plunges earthwards

1944-45 – DECLINE AND DISSOLUTION

Among this assemblage of captured Ju 88s and Ju 188s are aircraft of II./LG 1 which surrendered at Schleswig in May 1945

That same day saw the relief of Bastogne by US troops driving up from the south. But this did not stop the bombing. On the night of 29/30 December over 60 sorties were flown in two separate waves, I./KG 66 participating in both. It was the heaviest bombing raid carried out by the Luftwaffe during the entire Ardennes campaign.

Forty-eight hours later, on the last night of the year, LG 1 returned to Bastogne. They started fires which were still raging at dawn when the Luftwaffe' fighter arm staged its own last great folly in the west – the murderously expensive New Year's Day attack on Allied airfields.

With the total collapse of the Ardennes counter-offensive, there was little more that the Junkers *Kampfgruppen* in the west could do. Although their numbers were once again made good, supplies of aviation fuel, long critical, were by now almost non-existent. In March 1945 the pathfinders of I./KG 66 deployed briefly to the eastern front before staging northwards to Scandinavia to await surrender. LG 1 was to meet its end in northern Germany, I. *Gruppe* surrendering to Canadian forces at Varel in April and II. *Gruppe* to the British at Schleswig in May.

But there had been one final operation involving the Ju 88 in the west in that spring of 1945. On 7 March the US 1st Army had captured intact the bridge over the Rhine at Remagen. For ten days American troops poured across its weakened spans while German forces attempted with all the means at their disposal to destroy it.

After everything else had failed they called upon the *Mistel Gruppe*, by now redesignated a second time and currently heavily engaged on the eastern front as II./KG 200. Taking advantage of the bad weather in the Remagen area on 15 March, four *Misteln* were launched at the bridge. None hit.

Four Ju 88s . . . unmanned, stuffed with explosives, expendable. A sad end for the record-breaking *Wunderbomber*.

APPENDICES

REPRESENTATIVE Ju 88/188 BOMBER STRENGTHS IN THE WEST

A)   BLITZKRIEG – 10 MAY 1940

Luftflotte 1 HQ: Berlin		Base	Type	Est-Serv
II./KG 28	Maj Kaufmann	Kassel-Rothwesten	Ju 88A	4-2

Luftflotte 2 HQ: Münster

Fliegerkorps z.b.V 2				
III./KG 4*	Hptm Bloedorn	Delmenhorst	Ju 88A	37-21

IV. Fliegerkorps				
Stab (K) LG 1*	Oberst Bülowius	Düsseldorf	Ju 88A	2-2
II.(K) LG 1*	Maj Dobratz	Düsseldorf	Ju 88A	32-4
III.(K) LG 1*	Maj Dr Bormann	Düsseldorf	Ju 88A	37-12
Stab KG 30*	Oberstlt Loebel	Oldenburg	Ju 88A	2-2
I./KG 30	Maj Doench	Oldenburg	Ju 88A	34-25
II./KG 30	Hptm Hinkelbein	Oldenburg	Ju 88A	38-25
III./KG 30	Maj Crüger	Marx	Ju 88A	30-20

Luftflotte 3 HQ: Bad Orb

V. Fliegerkorps				
Stab KG 51*	Oberst Kammhuber	Landsberg/Lech	Ju 88A	1-0
I./KG 51*	Maj Schulz-Heyn	Lechfeld	Ju 88A	23-7
II./KG 51	Maj Winkler	München-Riem	Ju 88A	38-15

			Total	277-133

*Also equipped with He 111

B)   BATTLE OF BRITAIN – 13 AUGUST 1940

Luftflotte 2 HQ: Brussels		Base	Type	Est-Serv
I. Fliegerkorps				
II./KG 76	Maj Möricke	Creil	Ju 88A	36-28
KG 77	(Re-equipping)			
9. Fliegerdivision				
III./KG 4	Hptm Bloedorn	Amsterdam-Schiphol	Ju 88A	35-23
Stab KG 40	Oberstlt Geisse	Brest-Guipavas	Ju 88A	1-1

Luftflotte 3 HQ: Paris		Base	Type	Est-Serv
IV. Fliegerkorps				
Stab LG 1	Oberst Bülowius	Orléans-Bricy	Ju 88A	2-1
I.(K)/LG 1*	Hptm Kern	Orléans-Bricy	Ju 88A	33-23
II.(K)/LG 1	Maj Dobratz	Orléans-Bricy	Ju 88A	34-24
III.(K)/LG 1	Maj Dr Bormann	Chateaudun	Ju 88A	34-23
KGr 806	Hptm Linke	Caen-Carpiquet	Ju 88A	33-22
V. Fliegerkorps				
Stab KG 51	Maj Schulz-Heyn	Paris-Orly	Ju 88A	1-1
I./KG 51	Hptm von Greiff	Melun-Villaoche	Ju 88A	30-21
II./KG 51	Maj Winkler	Etampes-Mondésir	Ju 88A	34-24
III./KG 51	Maj Marienfeld	Etampes-Mondésir	Ju 88A	35-25
I./KG 54	Hptm Heydebreck	Evreux	Ju 88A	35-29
II./KG 54	Hptm Schlaeger	St André	Ju 88A	31-23
Luftflotte 5 HQ: Stavanger				
Stab KG 30	Oberstlt Loebel	Aalborg	Ju 88A	1-1
I./KG 30	Maj Doench	Aalborg	Ju 88A	40-34
III./KG 30	Hptm Kollewe	Aalborg	Ju 88A	35-27
			Total	**447-330**

*Also equipped with He 111

C) NORMANDY – 15 JUNE 1944

Luftflotte 3 HQ: Paris		Base	Type	Est-Serv
IX. Fliegerkorps				
Stab KG 2	Maj Schönberger (acting)	Couvron	Ju 188E	3-2
I./KG 2	Maj Schönberger	Couvron	Ju 188A	8-2
II./KG 2	Maj Engel	Couvron	Ju 188E	5-4
Stab KG 6	Oberstlt Hogeback	Melsbroek	Ju 88A	1-1
I./KG 6	Maj Fuhrhop	Brétigny	Ju 188A	16-11
III./KG 6	Maj Puchinger	Ahlhorn	Ju 188A	18-11
Stab KG 30	Oberstlt v Gravenreuth	Zwischenahn	Ju 88A	2-1
Stab KG 54	Oberstlt Riedesel Frhr. von Eisenbach Marx		Ju 88A	1-1
I./KG 54	Maj Sehrt	Wittmund	Ju 88A	16-9
III./KG 54	Hptm Brogsitter	Marx	Ju 88A	11-7
I./KG 66	Maj Schmidt	Avord	Ju 88S	6-5
			Ju 188E	3-0
II./KG 76	Maj Geisler	Melsbroek	Ju 88A	13-9
Stab LG 1	Oberst Helbig	Le Coulet	Ju 88A	1-1
I./LG 1	Maj Ott	Le Coulet	Ju 88A	23-14
II./LG 1	Maj Clemm von Hohenberg	Chievres	Ju 88A	23-19
2. Fliegerdivision (Southern France)				
Stab KG 26	Oberstlt Klümper	Montpellier	Ju 88A	1-1
II./KG 26	Maj Teske	Valence	Ju 88A	27-18
III./KG 26	Maj Thomsen	Montpellier	Ju 88A	22-12
			Total	**200-128**

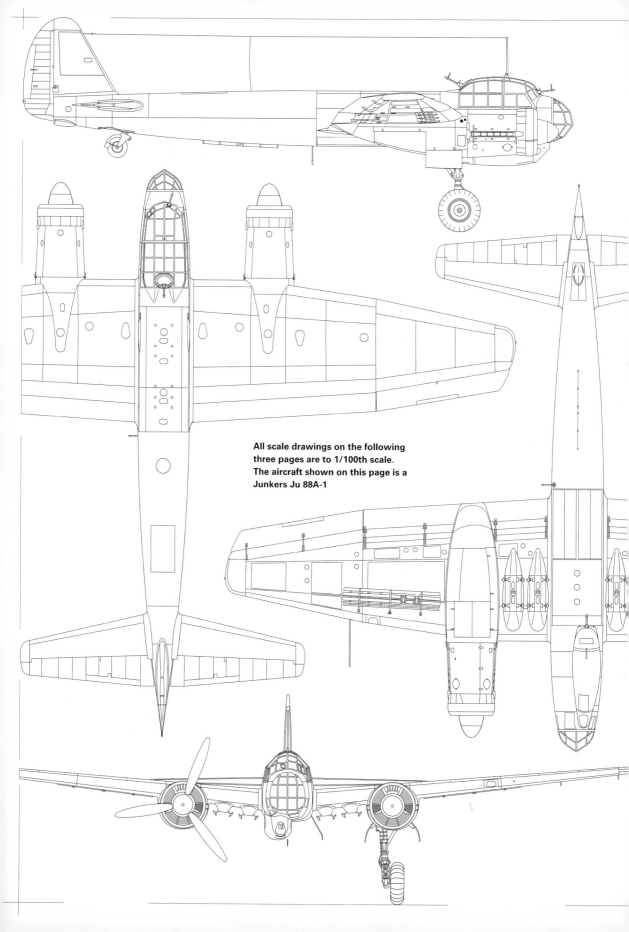

All scale drawings on the following
three pages are to 1/100th scale.
The aircraft shown on this page is a
Junkers Ju 88A-1

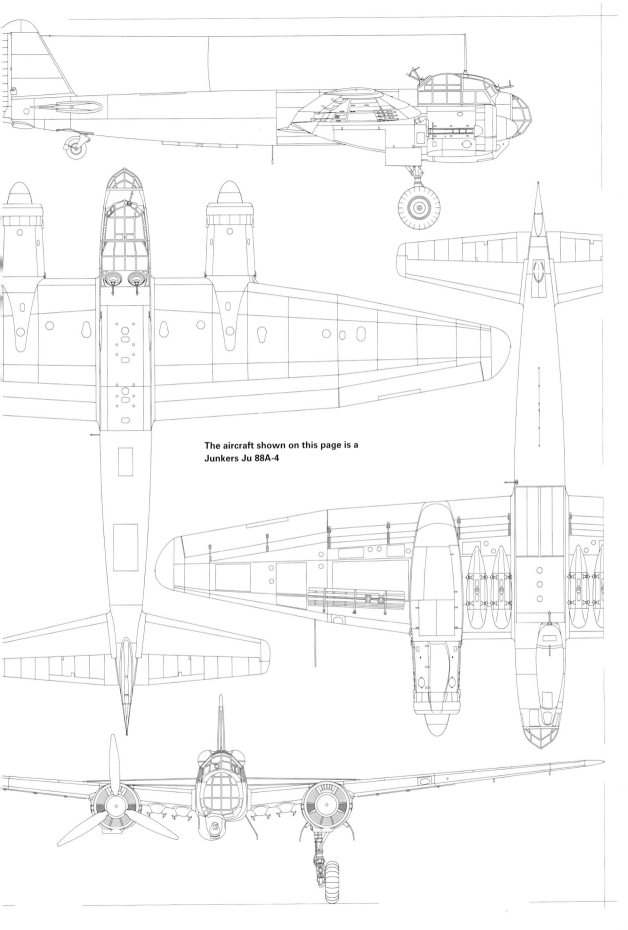

The aircraft shown on this page is a
Junkers Ju 88A-4

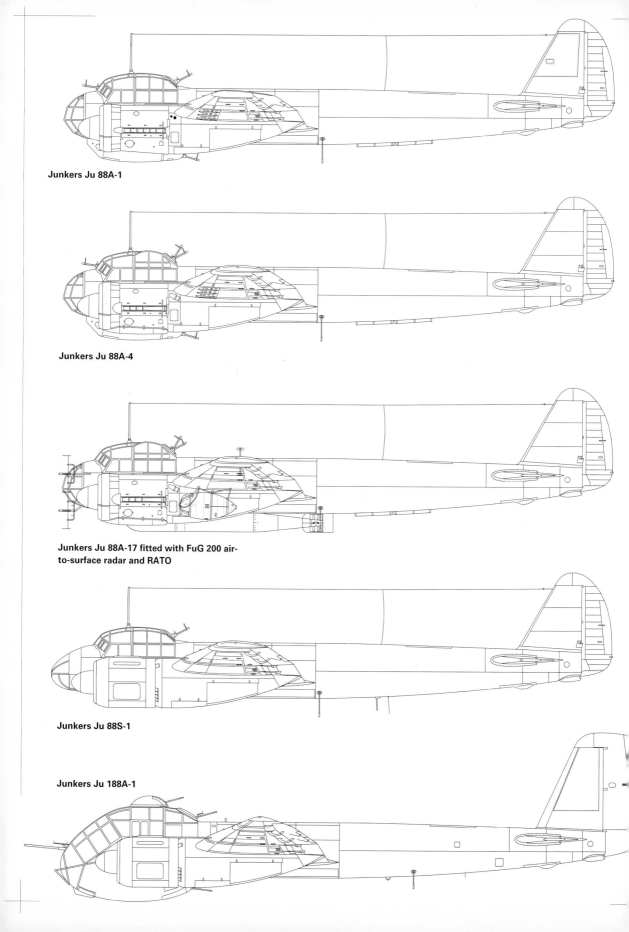

Junkers Ju 88A-1

Junkers Ju 88A-4

Junkers Ju 88A-17 fitted with FuG 200 air-to-surface radar and RATO

Junkers Ju 88S-1

Junkers Ju 188A-1

COLOUR PLATES

1

Ju 88A-5 'V4+LT' of 9./KG 1 'Hindenburg', Roye/Amy, April 1941

A typical example of the anonymity adopted by most Junkers *Gruppen* at the height of the night Blitz, III./KG 1's *'Theodor-Ludwig'* has had liberal amounts of washable black distemper applied to its undersides and over all markings and insignia. Only the small white 'LT' on the aft fuselage offers a clue as to its identity. However, most *Geschwader* and/or *Gruppen* were reluctant to overpaint their unit badges, and although hidden here, 'LT' carries the facsimile Hindenburg signature below the pilot's window (see photo page 64).

2

Ju 188E 'U5+EM' of 4./KG 2 'Holzhammer', Münster-Handorf, January 1944

When II./KG 2 re-equipped with the Ju 188E during the winter of 1943-44, its first machines wore this standard maritime-style finish of blue-grey meander over dark green. Note, too, the regulation national insignia and unit codes of the period.

3

Ju 188E 'CP' of 6./KG 2 'Holzhammer', Münster-Handorf, April 1944

Once committed to *Steinbock*, many II./KG 2 aircraft were provided with a camouflage scheme more suited to nocturnal operations – matt black undersides with blue-grey (RLM 76) upper surfaces, the latter broken up with a disruptive two-tone pattern. Fuselage crosses were narrow bordered, while the *Geschwader's* small 'U5' code lettering and the tailfin swastika were sometimes dispensed with altogether.

4

Ju 88A-1 '5J+CS' of 8./KG 4 'General Wever', Kirchhellen, June 1940

Wearing otherwise textbook finish, markings and insignia of the daylight *Blitzkrieg* in the west period, most of III./KG 4's early Junkers appear to have sported pre-war style narrow bordered fuselage crosses (as reintroduced towards the end of the war in conjunction with low-visibility camouflage schemes – see profile 3 immediately above for example). Note the aircraft's individual letter 'C' in red outlined in white, a colour combination repeated on the spinner tips.

5

Ju 188E '3E+EL' of 3./KG 6, Chievres, October 1943

I./KG 6's first Ju 188s were delivered in the late summer/ early autumn of 1943 in standard day camouflage finish, but were soon subjected to the same kind of treatment as had been meted out to their Ju 88 predecessors engaged in the night Blitz of 1940-4 1 – all light areas were quickly overpainted a sooty black. 3. *Staffel's* 'Emil-Ludwig' is well prepared for its next nocturnal foray over England.

6

Ju 188A-14 '3E+NS' of 8./KG 6, Melsbroek, February 1944

Unlike I. *Gruppe*, II. and III./KG 6 retained Ju 188s throughout the *Steinbock* offensive of early 1944. Wearing a basic night-bomber finish of dark green (70/71) top surfaces over black undersides, 'NS' has had spots of blue-grey 76 applied over all its upper surfaces – a not uncommon practice on III./*Gruppe* aircraft of this period. Note also the grey codes and toned-down, narrow-bordered fuselage cross.

7

Ju 88A-4 '1H+EW' of 12./KG 26, Westerland/Sylt, Summer 1942

Although several IV. *Gruppen* (which were 'quasi-OTUs') were pressed into service over England during the 1942 *Baedeker* offensive, IV./KG 26 was not among them. Its parent *Geschwader* had been selected as the Luftwaffe's specialist torpedo-bomber unit, and although the unit would later participate briefly in the Normandy campaign, its main areas of activity were the Mediterranean and the far north of Norway, where it fought against the Russian convoys. No sign of any practice torpedos here, but note the anti-shipping cannon in the nose of 'EW'.

8

Ju 88A-1 '4D+BA' of *Stab* KG 30, Trondheim-Vaernes, April 1940

Pictured during the campaign in Norway, this *Stabsstaffel* machine was presumably among the first delivered to KG 30, for it combines a narrow-bordered *Balkenkreuz* with the high demarcation line between upper and lower camouflage surfaces which was a feature of some of the earliest Junkers to enter service. Note also the *Geschwaderstab's* 'Diving eagle' badge displaying the colours of all three component *Gruppen* on its background shield.

9

Ju 88A-5 '4D+KL' of 3./KG 30, Aalborg, August 1940

KG 30 was based at Aalborg, in Denmark, for much of the Battle of Britain. This I. *Gruppe* machine (note plain white background to the *Geschwader* badge) was one of those which did not return from the disastrous 15 August raid across the North Sea, crash-landing near Bridlington after being attacked by a No 73 Sqn Hurricane I flown by Sgt A L McNay.

10

Ju 88A '4D+AD' of *Stab* III./KG 30, Eindhoven, September 1940

KG 30's transfer from *Luftflotte* 5 to *Luftflotte* 2 did not halt the losses. The yellow shield indicates that this machine belongs to III. *Gruppe*. In fact, as the fuselage code shows, it is the aircraft flown by *Gruppenkommandeur* Major Hackbarth (who also happened to be the son-in-law of *Luftflotte* 2's AOC, *Generalfeldmarschall* Kesselring), which was forced to ditch in shallow water off Pagham on 9 September after being attacked by Spitfires from No 603 Sqn.

11
Ju 88A '4D+GM' of 4./KG 30, Lister, March 1943
KG 30 subsequently returned to Norway, where it became heavily involved against the Arctic convoys. But it also put in the occasional appearance over the North Sea, attacking Britain's coastal shipping by night. This cannon-armed machine of II. *Gruppe*, with toned-down markings, temporary black undersides and exhaust shrouds, was on detachment to southern Norway and engaged in just such operations.

12
Ju 88A-1 '9K+AB' of *Stab* I./KG 51 'Edelweiss', Melun-Villaroche, August 1940
Another *Gruppenkommandeur* machine, this one flown by I./KG 51's Hauptmann Kurt von Greiff during the closing stages of the daylight Battle of Britain. Note the prominent white spinners (of I. *Gruppe*) and the narrow white band around the lip of the radiator cowling, the latter embellishment possibly denoting an aircraft of the *Stabskette*.

13
Ju 88A-1 '9K+GR' of 7./KG 51 'Edelweiss', Brétigny, November 1940
In stark contrast to the machine above, this 'blacked out' A-1 was obviously participating in the night Blitz. The temporary finish may have provided some protection in the darkness over England, but *'Gustav-Richard'* was fated to meet its end over France in daylight. It inexplicably exploded during a domestic flight near Paris on 18 November, killing Unteroffizier Meissner and his crew.

14
Ju 88A-1 '9K+EH' of 1./KG 51 'Edelweiss', Melun-Villaroche, Winter 1940-41
Variation on a theme – 1. *Staffel's* 'Emil-Heinrich' sports a different form of temporary night camouflage. The entire rear fuselage has been overpainted, with the aircraft's 'last two' then being re-applied in a very spidery form. But the crew almost paid the ultimate price for leaving the national insignia so visible. Their aircraft was severely damaged over England (whether by anti-aircraft fire or nightfighter is not known) and they were lucky to make it back to base, where the pilot pulled off a successful belly-landing.

15
Ju 88A-1 'B3+EH' of 1./KG 54 'Totenkopf', Evreux, August 1940
Representative of KG 54's aircraft at the height of the Battle of Britain, 'B3+EH' (Wk-Nr 4079) was another machine which later came to grief over

France. It crashed south-east of Rouen on 6 October 1940 after suffering engine failure while returning from a night raid on London. All four crew members baled out and survived.

16
Ju 88A-1 'B3+IM' of 4./KG 54 'Totenkopf', St André, Winter 1940-41
By the time of 'EH''s loss (above), KG 54 were also beginning to apply black distemper to their machines to render them less visible in their new nocturnal environment. *'Ida-Martha's'* crew have been more sparing with the paintbrush than most, being content merely to overpaint the glaring white of the national insignia and the aircraft's individual letter 'I'.

17
Ju 88A-4 'B3+PL' of 3./KG 54 'Totenkopf', Jever, April 1944
After more than two years in the Mediterranean theatre, I./KG 54 was recalled to northern Germany to participate in the *'Steinbock'* offensive. Wk-Nr 141214 was still resplendent in maritime camouflage (although the *Geschwader's* distinctive 'Death's head' badge had been painted out to hide evidence of the recent transfer) when it took off for London on the night of 18/19 April. Hit by AA fire over the capital (which knocked out the port engine and many of the flying instruments, including the compass), Unteroffizier Brandt struggled on for another ninety minutes in an effort to reach Holland before making a wheels-up landing on a dimly lit airfield . . . in Essex!

18
Ju 88S-1 'Z6+BH' of 1./KG 66, Avord, April 1944
Few units took the fine art of anonymity further than the pathfinders of I./KG 66. Engaged in the *Steinbock* offensive, this night-camouflaged Ju 88S has a dense dapple of dark grey spots over all blue-grey upper surfaces. The national insignia is still prominent, but the aircraft's four-digit code, 'Z6-BH', is almost lost high up on the tailfin to the right of the swastika. Note, however, that the individual letter 'B' is still painstakingly applied in the correct *Staffel* colour of white.

19
Ju 188E 'Z6-LH' of 1./KG 66, Montdidier, July 1944
Although in the same overall finish as the S-1 above, this Ju 188E – depicted at the height of the Normandy campaign – has had its fuselage *Balkenkreuz* toned down and the tail swastika obliterated altogether. Only the tell-tale gap among the dark grey spots on the tailfin reveals the whereabouts of the four-digit code which, being entirely in white on blue-grey, is otherwise all but indiscernible.

20
Ju 88S-3 'Z6+FH' of 1./KG 66, Dedesdorf, December 1944
Having survived Normandy, I./KG 66 retreated via

Belgium and Holland to northern Germany. By now it was also operating a small number of S-3s, most – if not all – of which were finished in overall black 76. Prior to the launch of the Ardennes counter-offensive, these aircraft were given a blue-grey 76 meander pattern over both upper and lower surfaces. This helped them to blend in against the wooded, snow-covered terrain of the area but, at the same time, effectively obscured all markings other than the individual letter on the fuselage side.

21
Ju 88A-5 'F1+BD' of *Stab* III./KG 76, Illesheim, February 1941

III./KG 76 was one of the last *Gruppen* to convert to the Ju 88 and see brief action in the west before the mass exodus eastwards in preparation for the invasion of Russia in June 1941. Wearing textbook finish and markings, this *Stabskette* machine sports tricolour spinners representing all three subordinate *Staffeln*. During its short stint of service flying Ju 88s over England, the *Gruppe* lost just five aircraft including *'Berta-Dora's'* sistership 'F1+AD', flown by Major von Ziehlberg, on the night of 7/8 May.

22
Ju 88A-5 'F1+BR' of 7./KG 76, Soesterberg, April 1941

Newly re-equipped, III./KG 76 flew its Ju 88s into Soesterberg towards the end of April 1941. *'Berta-Richard's'* glaring white *Staffel* markings (spinners, fuselage band and individual letter) were undoubtedly given a precautionary coat of black paint before the *Gruppe* first ventured across the North Sea into Britain's night skies early the following month . . .

23
Ju 88A-5 'F1+GS' of 8./KG 76, Soesterberg, April 1941

. . . which is presumably what has been happening here to 8. *Staffel's 'Gustav-Siegfried'*, although quite why the tailfin swastika has been overpainted and the 'last two' crudely daubed below it, while the fuselage markings (including the red *Staffel* band) have been left intact, is not quite clear. Perhaps operational requirements interrupted the work and the crew just had to take their chances?

24
Ju 88A-1 '3Z+BB' of *Stab* I./KG 77, Laon-Athies, October 1940

This *Stabskette* machine (Wk-Nr 4136) is the aircraft in which Oberleutnant Fiebig set out on 3 October to attack Woodley airfield near Reading, but which ended up being brought down by the ground-defences of the de Havilland aircraft works at Hatfield instead (see text). The crew chose to attack the latter site due to poor visibility over Reading. Note the spinners combining the green of the *Gruppenstab* with the white of I. *Gruppe*.

25
Ju 88A-1 '3Z+KN' of 5./KG 77, Laon-Athies, September 1940

Prior to Fiebig's solo effort, KG 77 had flown two very costly mass raids in September from which 19 of their aircraft had failed to return. The large white rectangles which had been applied to the rudders and port wing upper surfaces of many of these machines, ostensibly for purposes of formating and recognition in the air (and as displayed here by 5. *Staffel's 'Kurfürst-Nordpol'*), no doubt provided an equally useful sighting aid for the RAF fighters which intercepted them.

26
Ju 88A-5 'L1+XB' of *Stab* I./LG 1, Orléans-Bricy, January 1941

Although at first glance this aircraft appears to be a normal night-undersided A-5 of I./LG 1's *Stabskette* (as witness the fuselage code), the presence of the small 'diving eagle' badge on the radiator cowling of this machine hints towards something of a mystery. The bomber's true ownership is corroborated by LG 1's 'Griffon' badge below the cockpit (hidden here, but see photo on page 29). So, unless this is the first recorded instance of 'zapping' in the wartime Luftwaffe, one can only assume that the crew had previously served with KG 30 . . .

27
Ju 88A-1 'L1+AL' of 3./LG 1, Orléans-Bricy, August 1940

. . . no mystery here though. Bearing a full set of regulation markings, *'Anton-Ludwig'* was the mount of Oberleutnant Sodemann, *Staffelkapitän* of 3./LG 1, who would crash-land this machine near Chichester after suffering damage from both fighters and AA fire during a daylight reconnaissance mission on 21 September.

28
Ju 88A-5 'M2+HK' of 2./KüFlGr 106, Vannes, April 1941

Although technically still under the control of the Kriegsmarine, and operating as maritime reconnaissance *Staffeln* based on the French Biscay coast, the Ju 88-equipped 2. and 3./106 also participated in the night Blitz over the UK in the spring of 1941. Hence the blacked-out national insignia and exhaust flame dampers fitted to this machine, which also retains its anti-shipping nose cannon.

29
Ju 88D-1 'M2+CH' of 1./KGr 106, Morlaix, April 1942

Transferred to the Luftwaffe and redesignated *Kampfgruppe* 106, this unit nevertheless continued its anti-shipping and maritime reconnaissance activities, flying a mix of Ju 88A bombers and, as here, Ju 88D armed reconnaissance aircraft. Further proof of its coastal role is provided by the scoreboard of vessels bombed or sunk meticulously recorded on the rudder of *'Cäsar-Heinrich'*, which was itself brought down by a No 253 Sqn Hurricane II nightfighter (flown by Wt Off Y Mahe) east of York in the early hours of 30 April.

30
Ju 88A-4 'S4+ML' of 3./KGr 506, Holland, June 1941
KüFlGr 506 was also redesignated as an autonomous *Kampfgruppe* in April 1941. Mainly active along the East Coast from bases in the Low Countries, the unit flew both day and night missions. Judging from its neatly overpainted national insignia and black undersides, this machine was currently engaged in the latter.

Back cover
Ju 88A-1 'M7+CK' of 2./KGr 806, Caen-Carpiquet, October 1940
One of the earliest *Küstenfliegergruppen* to become a *Kampfgruppe* (in the winter of 1939/40), KGr 806 converted from its He 111s to the Ju 88 at the start of the Battle of Britain. After participating in the daylight offensive – in standard finish as here – the *Gruppe* subsequently operated over Great Britain by night, before staging eastwards for the invasion of the Soviet Union in early June 1941.

SELECTED BIBLIOGRAPHY

Adler, Maj H, *Wir Greifen England An!* Wilhelm Limpert-Verlag, Berlin, 1940

Balke, Ulf, *Der Luftkrieg in Europa (KG 2 im Zweiten Weltkrieg) (Vols 1 & 2)*. Bernard & Graefe Verlag, Koblenz, 1989-1990

Bekker, Cajus, *Angriffshöhe 4000: Kriegstagebuch der deutschen Luftwaffe*. Gerhard Stalling Verlag, Oldenburg, 1964

Bingham, Victor, *Blitzed! The Battle of France May-June 1940*. Air Research Publications, New Malden, 1990

Bongartz, Heinz, *Luftkrieg im Westen*. Wilhelm Köhler Verlag, Minden, 1940

Brütting, Georg, *Das waren die deutschen Kampfflieger-Asse 1939-1945*. Motorbuch Verlag, Stuttgart, 1974

Cull, Brian, *et al*, *Twelve Days in May*. Grub Street, London, 1995

Dierich, Wolfgang, *Kampfgeschwader 51 'Edelweiss'*. Motorbuch Verlag, Stuttgart, 1975

Dierich, Wolfgang, *Die Verbände der Luftwaffe 1935-1945*. Motorbuch Verlag, Stuttgart, 1976

Gundelach, Karl, *Kampfgeschwader 'General Wever' 4*. Motorbuch Verlag, Stuttgart, 1978

Kohl, Herrmann, *Wir Fliegen gegen England*. Ensslin & Laiblin, Reutlingen, 1941

Loewenstern, Erich v, *Luftwaffe über dem Feind*. Wilhelm Limpert-Verlag, Berlin, 1941

Matthias, Joachim, *Alarm! Deutsche Flieger über England*. Steiniger-Verlage, Berlin, 1940

Neitzel, Sönke, *Der Einsatz der deutschen Luftwaffe über dem Atlantik und der Nordsee, 1939-1945*. Bernard & Graefe Verlag, Bonn, 1995

Orlovius, Dr Heinz, *Die Deutsche Luftfahrt, Jahrbuch 1941*. Verlag Fritz Knapp, Frankfurt-a-M, 1941

Parker, Danny S, *To Win the Winter Sky: Air War over the Ardennes, 1944-1945*. Greenhill Books, London, 1994

Price, Alfred, *Blitz on Britain 1939-1945*. Ian Allan, Shepperton, 1976

Radtke, Siegfried, *Kampfgeschwader 54*. Schild Verlag, Munich, 1990

Ramsey, Winston G (ed), *The Battle of Britain Then and Now*. After the Battle, London, 1985

Ramsey, Winston G (ed), *The Blitz Then and Now (3 Vols)*. After the Battle, London 1987, 1988 and 1990

Rose, Arno, *Mistel: Die Geschichte der Huckepack-Flugzeuge*. Motorbuch Verlag, Stuttgart, 1981

Schellmann, Holm, *Die Luftwaffe und das 'Bismarck' Unternehmen im Mai 1944*. Verlag E S Mitler & Sohn, Frankfurt/M, 1962

Schmidt, Rudi, *Achtung-Torpedo Los! Der . . Einsatz des Kampfgeschwaders 26*. Bernard & Graefe Verlag, Koblenz, 1991

Schramm, Percy E (ed), *Kriegstagebuch des OKW (8 Vols)*, Manfred Pawlak, Herrsching, 1982

Stahl, P W, *Kampfflieger zwischen Eismeer und Sahara (KG 30)*. Motorbuch Verlag, Stuttgart, 1982

Wood, Derek with Dempster, Derek, *The Narrow Margin*. Arrow, London, 1969

Various magazines, periodicals and yearbooks, both contemporary and postwar